ENVIRONMENTAL HUMANITIES IN FOLKTALES

This work throws light on the areas of space and time, nature and culture, spirit and matter in the folktales that nurture systemic thinking. It identifies and explores motifs and patterns in select folktales that promote interconnectedness, interdependence, holism, synthesis, and circular pattern of life and examines the ecological relevance of folktales in fostering a systematic view of life.

The volume discusses why it is important to critically analyze alternative worldviews in order to find holistic solutions to contemporary global ecological issues. It sheds light upon Ecofemiotics as a discipline, a portmanteau of Ecofeminist Semiotics, and through a re-reading of folktales, it puts forward an innovative folktale typology which connects women with environment. The book discusses an ecofemiotic cyclical praxis at three levels:

- Promoting theory to practice through the analysis of folktales as Gaia Care Narratives using the Ecofemiotic framework.
- Enabling practice to theory, through a classroom experiment, observation, and inference.
- Envisioning theory to practice, through the identification of Gaia Care Principles and its multidisciplinary hands-on scope and function to create avenues toward ecological balance and sustainable living.

Inspired by the hearts that tell stories of love, care, nurture, and the Earth, this nuanced work will be of interest to students and researchers of literature and literary theory, sociology, social anthropology, gender studies and women's studies, feminism, development studies, environment, and folklore studies.

P. Mary Vidya Porselvi is Assistant Professor of English, Loyola College, Chennai, India. She obtained her BA, MA, and PhD degrees from Stella Maris College. Her primary research was on the topic "Mother Earth Discourse as Conscientizacao: An Ecofeminist Approach to Folktales from India", and she has identified an innovative folktale typology which connects women with environment. She has been a recipient of the Fulbright (FNAPE) Award for the year 2019–2020, and she worked on the topic "Indian Classical Ecocriticism: An Ecofeminist-Semiotic Study". She has authored books titled *Bhoomi Tales* (2015), *Nature's Voices Women's Voices* (2015), *Nature, Culture and Gender: Rereading the Folktale* with Routledge and Taylor and Francis (2016) and *Sylvan Tones: English through Folklore'* (2017).

Environmental Humanities in Folktales

Theory and Practice

P. Mary Vidya Porselvi

Routledge
Taylor & Francis Group

LONDON AND NEW YORK

First published 2023
by Routledge
4 Park Square, Milton Park, Abingdon, Oxon OX14 4RN

and by Routledge
605 Third Avenue, New York, NY 10158

Routledge is an imprint of the Taylor & Francis Group, an informa business

© 2023 P. Mary Vidya Porselvi

The right of P. Mary Vidya Porselvi to be identified as author of this work has been asserted in accordance with sections 77 and 78 of the Copyright, Designs and Patents Act 1988.

British Library Cataloguing-in-Publication Data
A catalogue record for this book is available from the British Library

ISBN: 978-1-032-30987-3 (hbk)
ISBN: 978-1-032-52435-1 (pbk)
ISBN: 978-1-003-40668-6 (ebk)

DOI: 10.4324/9781003406686

Typeset in Times New Roman
by Apex CoVantage, LLC

TO
GAIA AND ALL HER CHILDREN
WHO BELIEVE
IN
LOVE AND CARE

Contents

Foreword

I was raised in a culture strangely devoid of folktales: late twentieth-century North America. I grew up watching television and reading books – and spending time outside, playing sports and looking for animals in the creeks and forests near my home in small-town Oregon. In lieu of folktales, I had Mutual of Omaha's *Wild Kingdom*, a weekly TV series about intrepid white, male zoologists who traveled around the world capturing animals (such as Amazonian anaconda snakes – the anaconda episode remains in my memory with special vividness!) for research and for sharing with the public in zoos.

I also loved reading books about animals, wild and domestic. I think I particularly enjoyed books about boys and their dogs, such as *Where the Red Fern Grows* (1961) and *Sounder* (1969). And then, in my actual life, I tried to live out fantasies of having a deep relationship with other species, patrolling the neighborhood with my Norwegian elkhound at my side or sometimes with a bull snake, gathered from the woods near my elementary school, wrapped around my neck. The mothers of my childhood friends were particularly shocked when I showed up on their doorsteps wearing a snake around my neck.

For me, I realize now, interactions with local wildlife and with domestic animals were a way of making contact with the world. I didn't really have cultural stories guiding me toward such a yearning, nor was I led by any particular religious upbringing. It was not until many years later that I recognized, in hindsight, how my impulse to study and be in contact with – to *befriend* – other living beings could be construed as a quasi-spiritual desire to reconnect with the larger world.

When asked a few years ago to write a chapter on "Literature" for *The Routledge Handbook of Religion and Ecology* (2017), I turned to literary texts from several cultural traditions for examples of guiding or chastising stories, *teaching* narratives. William Stafford, who lived in Portland, Oregon, not far my hometown of Eugene, urges himself and his readers to "think!" and recognize "the splendor of our lives" while recounting the experience of bicycling home from his job as a college teacher, and his point seems to be that when we open our hearts to the vivid reality of a sentient world, we no longer feel alone and isolated. His moving poem about bicycling – "Maybe Alone on My Bike" – inspires me to feel interconnected with the world whenever I am biking, running, or walking through my town or anywhere I happen to be visiting. The other short texts I wrote about in that chapter, Native American Ofelia Zepeda's "It Is Going to Rain" and English poet Wilfred Owen's World War I piece "Dulce Et Decorum Est", are also poetic statements of attachment to nature and detachment from nation-state loyalties. I often refer to Zepeda's poem as a bioregional text, as it demonstrates how a local, rural person, deeply attuned to the patterns of her environment, can discern the presence or absence of rain more effectively than a city-bound, university-trained meteorologist. Owen's famous critique of war and blind loyalty to one's national flag, vividly, almost brutally, shows that humans are mortal animals, like all other living beings, and by driving home how we are not exceptional, he emphasizes our most profound loyalty to the earth and our bond with other species rather than to the shallowness of geo-politics.

In other words, I was raised on popular culture in the United States in the 1960s and 1970s, but somehow, I found myself gravitating toward TV shows and books that fed my nascent curiosity about the more-than-human world. Later, literary texts began to serve me in this way, reinforcing my love of nature and my attachments to the plants and animals around me. These works of popular culture and literature have shaped my view of the world – and I suspect the worldviews of many others – in lieu of folklore or folk stories.

So when I read a book like P. Mary Vidya Porselvi's learned study *Environmental Humanities in Folktales: Theory and Practice*, I find myself overwhelmed by the hollowness of my own background. In hindsight, I would have given a lot to have had access to what she calls "Gaia Care Narratives". Perhaps I found my way to the pop culture equivalents of such narratives, just by luck or by accident, but my parents and other adults did not appear to consciously steer me and other children I knew to these stories. We did not sit around the campfire – or the kitchen table – sharing such stories. What stories we told came from the daily newspaper and from our own daily lives, but I would have been challenged, as a child, to connect my own life story to larger cultural wisdoms, passed along through time-tested lore.

I greatly admire Dr. Porselvi's ability to "identify and map nature-centric folktales as ecological narratives", drawing upon examples from many different corners of the world, from numerous cultures and subcultures, and particularly emphasizing the wisdom of indigenous and rural communities. I immediately recognize the value of this work and how it adds immensely to the human wisdom that we will need if we are to overcome the ecological predicament, we have created for ourselves through our greedy and short-sighted exploitation of natural "resources" and our damaging of ecological systems necessary for the continuing of life on Earth.

Environmental humanities scholars, from Pramod K. Nayar in India to Sarah E. McFarland in the United States, are increasingly focusing on how to use their scholarship to direct readers toward vulnerability studies and narratives of extinction. McFarland's 2021 book *Ecocollapse Fiction and Cultures of Human Extinction* seeks to remind readers that we are not exceptional. The goal of her book, she writes, is to figure out "how to reject the impulse of human exceptionalism that pervades Western thought and much speculative fiction by exploring those few texts that engage with the potential of human species extinction" (3). By recognizing our own vulnerability to existential threats, such as global climate change, perhaps we can shift the direction of our modern societies toward more sustainable worldviews and lifeways.

If we had a deeper knowledge of folktales and if we took these tales to heart, it is likely we would not be in such a dire predicament.

Another essential aspect of Dr. Porselvi's study is its use of *Akam*, a central tenet of *Tinai* philosophy from southern India, as a primary lens through which to read and think about world folklore. By emphasizing *Akam*, with its focus on the themes of love and care, this project decenters Western cultural and environmental philosophy and shifts the priority to local, indigenous concepts – or at least away from the very Western vocabularies and conceptual structures, such as "self" and "other", "subject" and "object" – that have contributed to our exploitative relationship with the planet we inhabit. The vast majority of environmental humanities scholarship, I'm sorry to admit in 2022, is still beholden to the very patterns of Western, industrial, capitalist thought that have produced the problems we're striving to correct. It's as if we're trapped. *We're Doomed. Now What?* writes American author Roy Scranton in the title of his 2018 collection of essays on war and climate change.

The answer to "now what?" includes turning toward alternative worldviews and vocabularies, such as the worldviews revealed through the folktales Dr. Porselvi studies in this book and the vocabularies offered by *Tinai*. This is also a time that calls for creative combinations of helpful philosophies, such as the synthesis of ecofeminist theory and semiotics that Dr. Porselvi calls "ecofemiotics" and the bringing together of ecofemiotics and Deep Ecology that occurs in certain aspects of this project. Even in the retention of particular theories from the West and the application of these lenses, as well as *Tinai*, to help explain the virtues of traditional Gaia Care Narratives, Dr. Porselvi is implying that we live during an all-hands-on-deck time, calling into action all useable ideas to tackle the world's problems.

I grew up without the benefit of folktales, but today I find myself – and my society – greatly in need of the wisdom these tales provide. *Environmental Humanities in Folktales* is a helpful path toward such necessary stories.

Scott Slovic
University of Idaho, USA

Preface

Gary Snyder in his essay, "The Place, the Region, and the Commons" notes, "The heart of a place is the home, and the heart of the home is the fire pit, the hearth". The Tamil word *Akam* denotes "heart", "home", and "Earth". A Tamil film song in praise of the Earth goddess as an all-pervading energy in the universe goes, *Janani Janani jagam nee agam nee* (Mother Creator of the universe/all creatures, you are the universe, you are the *agam* meaning heart/home/Earth) *Jagath kaarani nee paripoorani nee* (You are the cause/the agent/the factor/the gene/the seed of creation of this universe, you are wholesome and complete). Thus, if *Prakriti* is considered the holistic life-affirming principle that characterizes *Bhoomi/Bhuvana*/Mother Earth/Gaia who brings together all the living creatures under her love and care, then there is certainly a greater possibility to envision the ubiquitous sacred connection between the heart, the hearth, and the Earth.

Why *Akam*? Love predominates *Akam* poetry. Women have a voice in *Akam* poetry. Nature is at the core of *Akam* poetry. It represents an organic well-established network and support system in terms of mothers, sisters, and friends. Women uphold interconnectedness (in their prime understanding of time and seasons), interdependence (in their indomitable faith in nature and culture), and intrinsic value (extraordinary respect for the sacredness of life). *Akam* is the fort and forte of women, mothers and daughters, sisters and friends. Through the identification of folktales as Gaia Care Narratives *Akam* represents an ungendered space that speaks for endangered species.

In his book, *Animate Earth – Science, Intuition and Gaia* Stephan Harding exclaims,

Traditional peoples all over the world have believed in an Earth mother who bestows life and receives the dead into her rich soil. The ancient Greeks called her Gaia, the earthly presence of *anima mundi*, the vast and mysterious primordial intelligence that steadily gives birth to all that exists. The great nourishing subjectivity – at once both spiritual and material – that sustains all that is.

Anima Mundi in Latin means "the soul of the world". The Sanskrit *Atman* and the Tamil *Akam* are equivalents of the soul, the spirit, and the sacred. *Akam* is the soul of the part, the living and nonliving beings on Earth and the soul of the whole, the all-pervading Gaia. The book is inspired by the hearts that tell stories of love and care. In her Foreword to Stephan Harding's book, *Animate Earth – Science, Intuition and Gaia* Lynn Margulis explains, "No matter our religious preconceptions or our particular straightjacket of socialization, of so-called education, we recognize emotionally and intellectually that not only do we come from the prodigious Earth, but that, alas, when our heart stops beating each of us will return to her" (8). The inherent intricate connection between the heart, home, and Earth is love and care. As I was reading Tamil *Cankam* literature I was enamored by the theme of love as a universal principle that makes the earth go around. Drawing inspiration from *Akam* poetics of the classical Tamil poetry this book throws light upon the three dimensions namely *Mutal*, *Karu*, and *Uri* that have shaped the proposed theoretical framework. Ecofemiotics a portmanteau of Ecofeminist Semiotics is identified as an "ecofeminist" alternative to Ecosemiotics. It is identified as a tool to study *Akam* as a conglomeration of woman's space, nature's space, and narrative space in folklore. The concept of *Akam* is central to ecofeminist-semiotics/ecofemiotics, fostered and nurtured by ecological, gender theories and Zen philosophies to study the integral relation among space-time, nature-culture, and spirit-matter in folktales across the world.

Twenty years ago, a rendezvous with the indigenous ecofeminist thought happened. Since then, this green quest has enlivened my thought processes to discover folktales as environmental discourse. During my PhD research I explored the possibility of re-reading folktales as Mother Earth Discourse by identifying an innovative folktale typology which connects women with environment. Using a beehive model I identified motifs, patterns, concerns, relationships, worldviews, consciousness, and expressions in Indian folktales. Years later I understood the need to return to my roots and revisit the Tamil classical theory of *Akam* as an ecofeminist philosophy with contemporary relevance and significance. Quite interestingly, I also found the concept of *Akam* congruent with Deep Ecology, systems theories, Zen Buddhist philosophies, and indigenous knowledge systems that acknowledge a culture integrated with nature.

Through the ecofemiotic study the folktales emerge as Gaia Care Narratives that represent the motifs of interconnectedness, interdependence, and intrinsic value of life. The exploration of Spatio-Temporal Relativity in folktales promotes Interconnectedness; Naturo-Cultural Density encourages Interdependence; Spirituo-Physical Gravity emphasizes Intrinsic Value; and Socio-Economic Parity contributes to Eco-Emergence. Hence, the study initiates a quest to reinvent life-affirming avenues toward socio-economic parity, sustainable living, and ecological balance. In an age of environmental crisis and economic chaos, the alternative worldviews represented in the folktales promise hope for the well-being of Gaia and all her children and a better society for future generations.

The book throws light upon an ecofemiotic cyclical praxis at three levels: promoting theory to practice through the analysis of folktales as Gaia Care Narratives using the ecofemiotic framework; enabling practice to theory, through a classroom experiment, observation, and inference; and envisioning theory to practice, through the identification of Gaia Care Principles and its multidisciplinary hands-on scope and function to create avenues toward ecological balance and sustainable living.

Acknowledgments

To the environment that nourished me and the people who nurtured me, the Gaia in our lives, I owe my deepest appreciation.

My heartfelt gratitude to Prof. Dr. Scott Slovic, Professor, University of Idaho, USA, for being an astonishing inspiration in the field of environmental humanities and for his inspiring foreword for the book.

I would like to acknowledge USIEF and Fulbright who sponsored me to do research on the topic, "Indian Classical Ecocriticism: An Ecofeminist-Semiotic Study" in 2019 which has finally resulted in the form of a book. A special note of thanks to Prof. Dr. Martha Ann Selby, a Tamil Sangam scholar who invited me to teach and do research in the Department of Asian Studies, School of Liberal Arts, University of Texas at Austin, Texas, USA, during the Fall semester 2019. I am grateful to Prof. Dr. Donald R. Davis, Jr., Chairperson of the Department of Asian Studies, and Dr. Mary Rader, librarian, South Asian Studies, PCL, University of Texas at Austin, Texas, USA, for their enormous support and encouragement. My heartfelt thanks to Laura Mondino and Gowthaman Ranganathan, housemates at Austin for making me feel at home and my Fulbright visit, an unforgettable experience.

I am grateful to all the amazing people who have shaped this meaning-making process of love and care, to name a few, Mother Teresa, Thich Nhat Hanh, Arne Naess, Stephen Harding, James Lovelock, Vandana Shiva, Wangari Maathai, Satish Kumar, Nirmal Selvamony, Lynn Margulis, Paulo Freire, and the entire corpus of Tamil *Cankam* poetry. I profoundly thank the eminent scientist and Deep Ecologist Fritjof Capra for giving me an opportunity to attend his "The Systems View of Life" course in Fall 2021, for his insightful lectures and valuable inputs on the inter-relation between systems thinking and environmental sustainability. Not to forget his inspiring words on the closing session, "life organizes itself in networks, life is regenerative, life is creative and life is intelligent".

Special thanks to Dr. Brenda Beck, Adjunct Professor, Department of Anthropology, University of Toronto, Canada, for introducing me to the world of Anishinaabe folklore which has become a significant part of the classroom experiment in this research. I would like to acknowledge Margaret Read

MacDonald for giving me permission to use her book *Earth Care: World Folktales to Talk About* as one of the primary texts in the study.

My sincere thanks to the Management of Loyola College and the faculty of the Department of English, Loyola College, Chennai, for their encouragement and support. A special note of thanks to Dr. M. Gautaman, Head, Department of Sociology, Loyola College, and his faculty for introducing me to the contemporary sociological theories that enabled me to draw the distinctive connection between the imaginary environmental tales and the actual ecological problems we face in the contemporary world. Heartfelt thanks to my PhD supervisor Dr. Thilagavathi Joseph who continues to guide me and challenge me to work harder and better in my research quest and for her valuable suggestions and critical comments on the book. Thanks to Ms. Shoma Choudhury and Ms. Shloka Chauhan from Routledge for their meticulous work, able support, and cooperation to make the book a reality.

I would like to acknowledge the support of my research scholars, my first critics and reviewers, and my postgraduate students who actively participated in the classroom experiment that helped me to put my theory into practice.

I owe immense gratitude to my family, Appa Prof Dr. S. J. A Packiaraj, Amma Nirmala, my sister Priya Prem, my brother Jaikumar, my husband Roy Arun, my boys Amal and Iniyan for their enormous support, warmth, care, love, and patience that keeps me going amidst the innumerable commitments and challenges undertaken at home, workplace, and research.

Glossary

Ahimsa	(Sanskrit) – Nonviolence
Akam	(Tamil) – Heart, Home, Earth; interior world in *Cankam* poetry; deals with love in union and separation
Akaram	(Tamil) – The first alphabet in Tamil language
Akilam	(Tamil) – Universe
Cankam	(Tamil) – Fraternity that promoted literature; ancient Tamil period
Gaia	(Greek) – Goddess of the Earth
Karupporul	(Tamil) – Land, water, flora, fauna, and lifeworld
Kurinci	(Tamil) – Mountainous region in ancient Tamil Nādu
Marutam	(Tamil) – Agricultural region in ancient Tamil Nādu
Mullai	(Tamil) – Forest region in ancient Tamil Nādu
Mutarporul	(Tamil) – Space, time, and seasons
Neytal	(Tamil) – Coastal region in ancient Tamil Nādu
Oikos	(Greek) – Home, Earth
Palai	(Tamil) – Arid dry region in ancient Tamil Nādu
Puram	(Tamil) – Exterior world in *Cankam* poetry; deals with courage, benevolence, and leadership of the kings
Shakthi	(Sanskrit) – Power; woman
Stree Shakthi	(Sanskrit) – Woman power
Tinai	(Tamil) – Food grain; A holistic system of the ancient Tamil Nādu
Ubuntu	(African) – Togetherness
Uripporul	(Tamil) – Relationships, connection

Introduction
Heart, Hearth, and Earth

The book provides us an opportunity to study the folktales as ecological narratives that represent themes and motifs of interconnectedness, interdependence, and intrinsic value of life. Interestingly, the Tamil word *Akam* signifies "the heart", "the hearth" or "the homestead", and "the Earth" or "the larger home". Veering toward the understanding of love as the predominant theme of Tamil *Cankam Akam* poetry, the study promulgates love and care motifs in folktales that quintessentially connect, interconnect, and reconnect the heart with the hearth/home and in turn with the Earth.

Realigning with the principles of sustainable living as a fundamental concern of environmental humanities the research draws inspiration from the *Akam* poetics to identify and map nature-centric folktales as ecological narratives in relation to the three seminal characteristics namely space-time continuum, nature-culture proximity, and spirit-matter relationship. The proposed ecofeminist-semiotic/ecofemiotic approach inspires us to look at folktales as Gaia Care Narratives.

The study throws light upon the human obligation of storytelling as a means to show love and care for the environment. We humans are a storytelling species, and this study emphasizes our role in telling stories as an act of "humanizing" the environment. The study proposes an *Akam*-inspired framework titled "ecofemiotics", a portmanteau of "ecofeminist semiotics". Through the ecofemiotic framework the research examines space-time proximity, nature-culture connection and spirit-matter relation in folktales as Gaia Care Narratives which contribute to socio-economic parity and ecological balance.

As a basic premise, ecofemiotics emphasizes the spirit of interconnectedness, interdependence, and intrinsic value of life. Quite specifically, the book helps us to identify and map motifs and patterns in world folktales that represent an alternative socio-economic order with the spirit of wellbeing, ecological balance, and sustainable view of life. The stories are drawn from different nature-centered indigenous and rural cultures across the world.

DOI: 10.4324/9781003406686-1

The Scope of the Earth-Centered Narratives

As conscious citizens of the planet, we humans are invited to take a seat in the giant circle to revisit the folktales and reweave them to nourish and nurture the environmental imagination for a better future. The major objectives envisioned in the study are: to identify an integrated eco-spiritual theory and practice to understand folktale as an environmental discourse; to recognize the scope of the proposed ecofemiotic framework to assess and map the earth-centered folktales from different cultures across the world; to examine the scope of folktales as Gaia Care Narratives fortified by the earth-centered philosophies of life; and to explore the praxis of eco-storytelling as a pedagogical process of consciousness-raising. The pertinent research questions raised in the study are:

- What are the different motifs and patterns of space-time represented in the folktales in terms of interconnectedness?
- What are the various motifs and patterns of nature-culture represented in the folktales in terms of interdependence?
- What are the diverse motifs and patterns of spirit-matter represented in the folktales in terms of intrinsic value?

Folktales emerge from the human heart, mind, and soul which characterize *Akam*. They begin and end with life-affirmation in a circular pattern.

Undeniably, the storyteller and the told are not the same at the end of the storytelling session. In a culture integrated with nature, the storyteller emphatically narrates the tale with mindfulness and with a heart filled with love, care, concern, compassion, and sense of goodwill. Without a doubt, people who listen to the stories with mindfulness and with a caring heart become paramount agents of change. The study throws light upon motifs and symbols of: care, abundance, interconnectedness, rejuvenation, and circular pattern of life; mindfulness, meditation, knowledge, and enlightenment; care, kindness, interdependence, refuge, and sacredness/intrinsic value; pluralism, networking, diversity, and collective identity; abundance, benevolence, and wellbeing; creativity, innovation, balance, and emergence. Quite specifically, the ecofemiotic study attempts:

- To identify motifs and patterns that represent alternative space-time fortified by interconnectedness and circular principles of time.
- To recognize the significance of green narratives with nature-culture proximity marked by interdependence.
- To examine folktales that uphold spirit-matter relationship characterized by intrinsic value or inherent worth.

Folklore is an essential expression of a group. Folktales represent the cultural fervor of a community. "Folk culture refers to the culture of ordinary

Introduction 3

people, particularly those living in pre-industrial societies . . . it arises from the grassroots, is self-created and autonomous and directly reflects the lives and experiences of the people. Examples of folk culture include traditional folk songs and traditional stories that have been handed down from generation to generation" (Haralambos and Holborn 727). The texts chosen for study include fables, parables from different cultures and spiritual traditions, myths and legends from different indigenous cultures, fairytales, and other indigenous anthologies. A fable is a short imaginary narrative that typically conveys a moral with animals and birds as characters. Aesop who lived during the sixth century is claimed to be a slave from the island of Samos. His fables have universal themes with time-tested values that mostly feature nonhuman life. Folklorists believe that fables were popular in Greece and India at the same period. The fables chosen for the study were retold by Joseph Jacobs. Though Aesop's tales are considered anthropomorphic in outlook, an interpretation lends itself to the understanding of Earth-centered ideals inherent in them. Fables portraying kindness, gratitude, goodwill, benevolence, and peaceful coexistence are highlighted during this study. Parables are short allegorical tales with a message embedded in them. Spiritual thinkers and visionaries often communicate with people through parables. Humans tend to draw relevant morals and messages from them to suit their lived experiences. Myth is an imaginary story that describes practices, beliefs, or a natural phenomenon, for example, creation myths and religious myths. Legend is a story from the past about a famous and important person in a particular culture. Myths and legends feature nature as their center. The creation myths and legends provide an alternative perspective to view the world. Legends of humans and their relation to the nonhuman subjects of nature celebrate the ecological faith in interdependence, interconnectedness, and intrinsic value of life.

Folktales are chosen from *Earth Care: World Folktales to Talk About* by Margaret Read Macdonald. They highlight earth-centered themes and motifs. Macdonald categorizes the stories under topics such as "Caring for our Land", "Caring for Our Forests", "Caring for Our Wetlands", "Caring for Our Creatures", "All Things Are Connected", "Our Place in Earth's Sacred Space", "No Thing Is Without Value", "The Folly of Human Greed", "Pollution Returns to the Polluter", "Planning for the Future", "The Wisdom of the Elders", "Many Voices Bring Results", and "One Person's Dream Can Make a Difference". Folktales portray an ideal imaginary space where nature becomes an agency. The study of folktales would create new avenues toward the understanding of sensitive humans who live close to nature. Folktales are chosen from *Gadi Mirrabooka: Australian Aboriginal Tales from the Dreaming* by Helen F MacKay, stories and folktales collected through fieldwork. An Anishinaabe folktale narrated by Kathleen Westcott was used in the classroom storytelling experiment.

Ecofeminist-Semiotic Methodology

A folktale is a sign of love. A symbol of care. A mark of faith. The storyteller is an icon of courage. The listeners are symbols of hope. In this study, semiotics is used as a methodology to study the signs and symbols in folktales in relation to space-time, nature-culture, spirit-matter, and in turn society-economy. Semiotics is the study of signs. As the framework draws inspiration from the earth-centered philosophies that work in favor of Gaia and all her children, the proposed theory can be called as Ecofemiotics. According to Julia Kristeva there are two modes of signification. "(1) as an expression of clear and orderly meaning and (2) as an evocation of feeling or, more profoundly, a discharge of the subject's energy and drives" (15–16). Folktales as Gaia Care Narratives underscore the second aspect as an impetus to identify and implement storytelling as a form of environmental signification.

Ecosemiotics is the study of signs in relation to Nature and Culture. Tracing the history of semiotics to Saussure's dyadic model of semiotics where the sign consists of a signifier and signified, Peirce formulated a three-part triadic model consisting of an interpretant, representamen, and an object. Later, Peirce recreated the ecosemiotic model with the three dimensions: text as a sign, the object in an environment, and the interpretant which includes the contextual meaning of the landscape. According to Siewers, Ecosemiotics grew from roots in nineteenth- and early twentieth-century American pragmatism and biological studies in Europe's eastern Baltic region, and the Native American cultural values indirectly helped to shape Peirce's Pragmatism (8). Subsequently, drawing inspiration from ecosemiotics, ecofemiotics attempts to make meaning out of the connection between the natural world and human understanding with the principles of love and care that characterize *Akam*. The syllable "fem" in Ecofemiotics denotes the ecofeminist turn to semiotics in unraveling folktales as Gaia Care Narratives and interestingly serves as an acronym to "first earth mindfulness", "first earth mediation", "first earth mapping", "first earth manifesto", and "first earth mission" envisioned by the eco-praxis to promote alternative environmental imagination.

Simply put, to identify an earth-centered folktale and telling it becomes an ecological meaning-making process. As Thomas Sebeok explains, "the phenomenon that distinguishes life forms from inanimate objects is 'semiosis'" (3). According to him there are six types of signs: the "symptom" which refers to intellectual, emotional, and social phenomena; the "signal" that indicates bird and animal signals and human signals and signaling systems for social purposes. The next three types of signs are "icons", "indexes", and "symbols" from Peirce's classification of signs. As Peirce puts it, "the universe . . . is perfused with signs, if it is not composed exclusively of signs" (10). There is no escape from signs. Those who cannot understand them and the systems of which they are a part are in the greatest danger of being manipulated by those who can. In short, semiotics cannot be left to semioticians (225). Ecofemiotics attempts to revisit the earth-centered tales and decode signs and symbols that contribute to the wellbeing of Mother Earth/Gaia and all her children. Through the analysis of ecological signs and symbols the study attempts to draw the connection between imagination and reality. Timo Maran and Kalevi Kull note, "what we provide here is not a Romanticist view to interpret nature as a text. Instead, it is a realist view that describes perceptual processes as sign processes and the actions in modifying the world on the basis of sign relations or codified representations" (42).

The key principles of ecosemiotics are: (1) The structure of ecological communities is based on semiosic bonds which talks about "most inter-species and intra-species relations – of which all ecological communities are composed – are based on sign relations" (Maran and Kull 43) and where "life and semiosis are coextensive" (Maran, Timo & Kalevi Kull 44). "Changing signs can change the existing order of things". (2) Living organisms change their environment on the basis of their own images of that environment where "Organisms can act only towards those objects in the environment that they do perceive and recognize. This means that acting towards the environment is critically dependent upon the distinctions that organisms are able to make" (Kull and Maran 44). (3) Semiosis regulates ecosystems. Meaning-making both stabilizes and destabilizes them where "The semiosic activities of ani-mals can provide regulatory functions that often have an integrative and sta-bilizing effect on ecosystems" (Kull and Maran 44). (4) "Human symbolic semiosis (with its capacity of de-contextualization) and environmental deg-radation are deeply related" (Kull and Maran 45). (5) Energetically and bio-geo-chemically, human culture is a part of ecosystem. Semiotically, culture is both a part and a meta-level of the semiosic ecological network (Kull and Maran 45). (6) The environment as a spatial-temporal manifestation of an eco-system functions as an interface for semiotic and communicative relations. (7) "Narrative description is inadequate for the description of ecological semiosis where narratives assume the involvement of language, since the syntactic ele-ments that are necessary for the description of a sequence of events as a whole require symbols" (Maran, Timo & Kalevi Kull 46). (8) The concept of culture is incomplete without an ecological dimension where "a theory of culture is incomplete without the eco semiotic aspect. Culture is the life of symbolic relations, of language capacity and meta descriptions. Culture is always part of an ecosystem and it never functions without non-linguistic sign systems, that is, without the non-cultural aspects of ecosystems and the semiosphere" (Maran, Timo & Kalevi Kull 46). Given these points, Ecofemiotics attempts to examine the symbolic relations in terms of space-time unity, nature-culture affinity, and spirit-matter harmony that govern an earth-centered way of life.

Above all, humans are an image-making, symbol-making species. They create, interpret, and derive meaning out of images and symbols in their day-to-day lives. Ecofemiotics is a method of understanding how and why we as human beings interact with other living beings and the environment. Scott

Slovic in his editor's preface to *Ecocriticism: Big ideas and Practical Strategies* explains "It all boils down to animality and place, two of the defining dimensions of our human existence – and the idea that media of cultural expression (poetry, painting, music, food, architecture, and so forth) represent our deepest thinking about these vital aspects of our lives" (Rangarajan vii). Storytelling also seeks to represent the connection between animality and place. As GN Devy elaborates,

> In an animate world, consciousness meets two immediate material realities: space and time. We put meaning into space by perceiving it in terms of images. The image-making faculty is a genetic gift to the human mind-this power of imagination helps us understand the space that envelopes us. In the case of time, we make connections with the help of memory.
>
> (xi)

Thus, the major characteristics of Gaia Care Narratives that emerge from the ecofemiotic study are: the semiotic process begins with the ecofeminist idea of Gaia or Mother Earth as a benevolent organic living being as a thought and praxis that leads on to conscientious action in terms of both sustainable balance and gender equity; all living beings and nonliving things are intricately connected to one another and form parts of the whole where the mapping of subjects in nature occurs by examining signs and symbols in the human narrative discourse. Both humans and nature are considered as "inter-beings" contributing to life-affirming meaning-making process; the meaning-making process of ecofeminist motifs and patterns contributes to the spirit of interdependence among all living beings. The anthropocentric viewpoints are interrogated by the idea of Deep Ecology where each and every life form on this planet has intrinsic value or inherent worth; the mapping of motifs and patterns happens with the understanding of nature-centered space-time, earth-centered nature-culture, life-centered spirit-matter, and a balanced society-economy; the connection between reflective thoughts and conscientious action is envisioned by the mindful storytellers who decode and recode nature-centered folktales as Gaia Care Narratives.

Structure of the Book

The book is divided into four chapters. Chapter 1 introduces *Akam* as an ecological philosophy. It begins with an introduction to the three-dimensional concept of *Akam* as the starting point of this study. It moves on to the theme of love as an organizing principle of *Akam* which fortifies and nourishes the proposed framework. *Akam* poems that celebrate the theme of love are analyzed in this section. Subsequently, care is identified as a unifying principle. This section draws a connection between *Akam* poetics, the indigenous

Anishinaabe philosophies, eco-critical theories such as deep ecology and ecofeminism, systems theories, and Zen philosophy.

Chapter 2 draws the inherent connection among the mindscape, story-scape, and signscape through the ecofemiotic framework to identify folk-tales as Gaia Care Narratives. The three major dimensions of the ecofemiotic framework are: spatio-temporal relativity reflecting the *Akam* concept of *mutal* (meaning "first"), referring to time, seasons, and space; nature-cultural density representing the *Akam* concept of *karu* (meaning "embryo") signifying flora, fauna, and the lifeworlds; and spirituo-physical gravity indicating the *Akam* concept of *Uri* (meaning "relationships") representing interconnections in the lifeworld. Based on the value of the three-dimensional paradigm folktales are categorized into eight types of *Akam* namely: celebrative *akam*, divisive *akam*, passive *akam*, oppressive *akam*, interactive *akam*, collaborative *akam*, transformative *akam*, and regenerative *akam*.

Chapter 3 deals with the analysis and synthesis of folktales as Gaia Care Narratives. The folktales are analyzed as Gaia Care Narratives under three sections namely: Space-Time continuum which deals with the motifs of inter-connectedness and cyclical pattern of life in select folktales; Nature-Culture proximity which unravels signs of interdependence in the chosen narratives; and Spirit-Matter connection in relation to the inherent worth of life in the chosen tales.

Chapter 4 provides an account of storytelling as eco-pedagogy based on a classroom experiment using an Anishinaabe folktale. *Akaram*, the integration of *Akam* (interior) and *Puram* (exterior), is the consciousness-raising space identified for storytelling in the classroom. Eco-storytelling is identified as an environmental praxis envisioned in five stages namely: mindfulness, mediation, mapping, manifesto, and mission, which result in the identification of the fourth dimension namely socio-economic parity.

The conclusion chapter titled "Multiverse in a Grain" signifying the undisputable potency of a folktale as seeds of consciousness includes the summing up, findings, recommendations for future study, and the identification of 40 Gaia Care Principles under the four categories: spatio-temporal relativity, naturo-cultural density, spirituo-physical gravity, and socio-economic parity.

The following chapter throws light upon *Akam* as an Ecological Philosophy.

1 *Akam* as an Ecological Philosophy

The Three-Dimensional *Akam*

The study identifies the three-dimensional *Akam* as an Ecological Philosophy akin to Deep Ecology and Ecofeminism. The proposed eco-critical approach draws sustenance from *Akam* poetry. The structural constituents of *Akam* poetry according to Tolkappiyam are *mutarporul, karupporul,* and *uripporul. Mutarporul* deals with time and seasons in relation to the land. In other words, *mutarporul* means, first, basic, fundamental aspects such as "Space and Time". *Karupporul* meaning the embryo, the fetus or the core "elements of the Landscape". The physical features of the land are seen in relation to God, food, animal, tree, bird, and occupation (Murugan 379). *Uripporul* refers to proper and specific "Relationships". *Akam* poetics lends itself to the connection between personal love and universal care.

Evolution of Thought

Tinai theory is a classical earth-centered philosophy that represents the society and culture of Tamil people during the *Cankam* period. In the modern era it is considered as an eco-critical philosophy popularized by Dr. Nirmal Selvamony in the west that throws light upon the human-nature kinship in Tamil poetry. *Tinai* is an order of community life found among early Tamils and, perhaps, others. Its characteristic feature is its emphasis on land-life relationship. Accordingly, human communities were organized on eco-regional basis (*Tinai* Studies by Dr. Selvamony). *Tinai* does not have an equivalent in English. It refers to the human–nature relationship inclusive of landscape, flora and fauna, and the way of life. *Akam* (meaning interior) and *Puram* (meaning exterior) are the two major dimensions of *Tinai*.

Nature is at the center of *Akam*. According to Tolkappiyam, *Akam* poetry represents the multidimensional aspects of land, water, flora, fauna, and the lifeworld. The five geographical regions in *Akam* poetry are: *kurinci*, hilly tract; *mullai*, forest tract; *marutam*, cultivable land; *neytal*, littoral tract; and

DOI: 10.4324/9781003406686-2

palai, arid dry land. The landscape is named after the characteristic flower of the region. The physical features of land include "God, food, animal, tree, bird, drum, occupation, and lute" (Murugan 379).

The poetic attributes of the five types of landscape are listed in the following section: The mood of the lovers in: *kurinci* is union of lovers; *mullai,* heroine expresses patient waiting over separation; *marutam,* lovers' quarrels, wife's irritability (husband accused of visiting a courtesan); *neytal,* heroine expresses grief over separation; *palai,* elopement, longest separation, dangerous journey by the hero. In terms of time and seasons, *kurinci* represents winter/cool and mist weather, and the time is midnight. In *mullai* the predominant time is evening, and the season is late summer, cloudy and rainy days. In *marutam* the time is dawn, early morning and no specific season. In *neytal* it is evening time/dusk and does not conform to any specific season. In *palai* it is noon time and set in the summer season.

To give a glimpse into the world of *Akam* ethos, the fauna in *kurinci* include monkey, bull, peacocks, parrots, and bees; in *mullai* it is elephant and deer; in *marutam* it is water buffalo, freshwater fish, and heron; in *neytal* it is crocodile and shark; in *palai* it is fatigued elephant, tiger, or wolf. The characteristic flora is jackfruit and *venkai* in *kurinci*; *konrai* and bamboo in *mullai*; mango in *marutam*; *punnai* in *neytal*; and cactus in *palai.*

In this era of environmental degradation, exploitation, and depletion, water is the most valuable resource. The water body in *kurinci* is mainly waterfalls, in *mullai* it is rivers, in *marutam* it is pond, in *neytal* it is well and sea, in *palai* it is dry wells and stagnant water. The characteristic soil in the five landscapes is red and black soil in *kurinci,* red soil in *mullai,* alluvial soil in *marutam,* sandy and saline soil in *neytal,* and dry land in *palai.*

People who live close to nature believe in work that contributes to sustainable living and ecological balance. In terms of occupation the women and men in *kurinci,* the mountainous region, gathered honey and grow millets; *mullai,* the forests, they had pastoral and agricultural work; the agricultural land, *marutam,* had farmers and peasants; in the coastal areas *neytal,* the fisherman sold fish and salt; and in palai, the dry arid land there were wayfarers and bandits. The *Akam* cosmos was characterized by eco-spirituality and their gods and goddesses represented the principles of nature. Murugan (meaning beauty) was the god of *kurinci*; Mayon, the god of rain protected *mullai*; Ventan, meaning *king* the god of *marutam*; Katalon, the god of the sea guarded *neytal*; and *Kotravai* (akin to durga/*shakthi*) who safeguarded people in times of trouble was the goddess of *palai.*

The poetic attributes of *Akam* poetry underscore the pertinent idea of the heart/soul as an all-encompassing phenomenon that connects the mindscape with the landscape. In the present times, we may classify the land, water, flora, and fauna as characteristics of *Puram,* or the exterior world. But the ancient Tamil people believed that humans were part of the larger environment and together they formed the *Akam,* the interior world.

Love as an Organizing Principle

The *Akam* concept of love that connects the heart with the home and the larger Home, the Earth can be seen as an underlying principle of the proposed eco-spiritual attitude of life. According to Kamil Zvelebil, "each poem celebrates the joy and delight of the created universe" (*Literary Conventions in Akam Poetry* v). *Tinai* is a holistic system that incorporates the entire socio-cultural milieu of ancient Tamil people into its realm. In the Tamil *Cankam Akam* poetry, the nonhuman living beings and nonliving beings are seen as life forms who have an equal role to play in the functioning of the planet. For example, in *Kuruntokai* Poem 40, Cempulap Peyanirar celebrates human love in relation to the harmonious integration of the elements of nature. The hero exclaims, "your mother and my mother, /how are they related? / Your father and my father, / what are they to/one another? / You and I, / how do we know each other? / Like the rain/and red earth, /our loving hearts are mingled/as one" (Balakrishnan 53). In this poetic narrative, the "rain" and "red earth" are signs of organic love and rejuvenation. Correspondingly, abundance and unconditional love form the core of eco-spirituality.

Love and care are unifying principles that connect space-time, nature-culture, and spirit-matter in this study. Poem 3 of *Kuruntokai* by Tevakulattar underscores the human perception of the environment in relation to her/his home and the "exterior" world. It highlights the heroine's eternal love for the hero. She metaphorically exclaims that her love is "wider than this earth, higher than the sky and unfathomably deeper than the sea!" (Balakrishnan 5). Similarly, In *Kurinci* poem 373, Maturai Kollan Pullan compares true love to the elements in nature. "My friend/The earth may change its position;/ Water and fire may change their properties too; / The vast ocean of shining waves may go dry;/ But our kinship with the lord of the high-peaked mountain/ Will never die for fear . . ." (Balakrishnan 518). The poem represents the human understanding of the environment in relation to her/his home and the "exterior" world. The earth, sky, and the ocean as elements of nature signify magnitude and abundance. Similarly, the ecofeminist philosophies reflect this connection as, "people ask me if I believe in the Goddess. I reply, 'Do you believe in the rocks?' . . . we connect with Her; through the moon, the stars, the ocean, the earth, trees, animals, through other human beings, through ourselves. She is here. She is within us all" (Gottlieb 318). The worldview of people who live close to nature is one of abundance. For example, in hills and forests, as noted by the natives of Kodaikanal, a hilly town in Tamil Nadu, people consume about half the number of fruits from trees for their daily use. They leave the balance for hungry travelers who travel that way. Travelers eat only to satisfy their hunger and leave the rest on the trees. Those remaining fruits are consumed by birds and animals like bats and squirrels. The world-view of abundance is characterized by this sense of contentment. It leads to a custom of sharing resources with the fellow living beings on earth.

The recognition of Mother Earth as a living, loving being and a nurturer has both positive and negative consequences on women and other marginalized groups. In poem 158 of Kuruntokai, Auvaiyar begins with the Ecofeminist metaphor, "O great rain clouds, pregnant/ with child, approaching/with winds mixed with the roaring voice/ of thunder, who frighten snakes/on the slopes of long mountains:/you have a character strong enough to shake the glorious Himalayas. / What is this? /Have you no pity for poor women/separated from their men?" (Balakrishnan 203). These lines indicate the power of Gaia inherent in all human beings especially women who revere and protect nature and their environment around them.

In the *Akam* poems, nature, culture, and the sacred are intrinsically connected with one another. Humans converse with other living beings on sublime thoughts like love and eternity. The hero speaks to the bees, the heroine speaks to the birds, and so on. Love is a guiding principle to measure the height, depth, and width of the entire space. Women share a loving relationship with humans and nonhumans despite their differences. They help one another and support them in times of need and suffering. The symbols in the Tamil *Cankam* poems denote organic love. Humans learn abundance from bees, mountains, and forests, benevolence from clouds and rain, and hope and strength from bamboo and elephants.

The sacred within the *Akam* manifests itself to the sacred in the universe. A heart filled with abundance, the *Akam* is an organic cosmos which unites the sky and the earth on one level and flora, fauna, and the lifeworld as kith and kin on another level. By juxtaposing the ecological crisis and environmental chaos of the contemporary times that have resulted from consumerism and commodification, fragmentation and reductionism, monoculture, and a worldview of scarcity with the alternative worldviews of wellbeing, subsistence, ecological balance, and a sustainable perspective, the proposed ecofemiotic approach creates a roadmap with alternative earth-centered worldviews and eco-critical consciousness. The study challenges the dominant ideologies of the Anthropocene era that have contributed to the ecological and economic chaos to re-bridge the dichotomies that separate nature and culture, man and woman, self and the other, mindscape and the landscape, humans and nonhumans, and home and the outside world. The storytelling process as eco-pedagogy envisions a radical reshaping of dominant worldviews that are in antithesis to the indigenous worldviews across the world.

All things considered, *Akam* is identified as an eco-critical tool for mapping socio-cultural-geographic-economic-semiotic aspects in the folktales. Human beings are endowed with a distinct quality to revere the sacredness/ intrinsic value of life on this planet and the larger universe and express them in their stories. Human thought and action have a major impact on the environment. There is a direct connection among the heart (*Akam*), the home (*Akam*), and the planet (*Akam*) characterized by abundance. Each living being and nonliving thing as parts of a whole serve a specific purpose in the peaceful coexistence of the planet.

All living beings possess the consciousness of the supreme power of nonviolence and peace within their *Akam* in congruence with Mother Earth. *Akam* is a holistic way of understanding the harmonious relation between the microcosm and the macrocosm. Without a doubt, *Akam* seeks to acknowledge the *Akam* (heart) of the tiniest insect, plant, or rock in the planet and in the universe. As a result, *Akam* fortifies the dynamics of *Puram*. *Akam* represents the home and the family. *Akam* poetry deals with familial relationships and kinship. Interestingly, the personae in *Akam* poetry are: woman in love, the heroine who is called *talaivi* or *kilatti*; man in love, the hero who is called *talaivan* or *kilavan*; hero's friend, *pankan*; who functions mainly as the hero's listener and is often described as a charioteer of the hero; woman's friend, *tozhi* or *panki* who is the daughter of the foster mother of the heroine and her closest friend and is sympathetic toward the heroine's love affair; heroine's mother *Narray* and her foster mother *Cevili taai*; and courtesan *parattai* or *kamakilatti*. In *Akam* poetry there is a speaker (*kurru*) and listener/listeners (*ketpor*). Each poem has a short narrative within itself. Therefore, *Akam* reflects the holistic principles and dynamics of Mother Earth. Human beings are conscious of the nonhuman life around them.

Akam as the heart, the hearth, and the earth provides an organic connection to the family. Stories begin at home in the family. Family is regarded as the basis of society. The structure of a family differs from culture to culture. Folktales represent different types of families. The sociologist Murdock argues that "the family performs four basic functions in all societies. These universal functions he terms the sexual, reproductive, economic and educational. They are essential for social life since without the sexual and reproductive functions there would be no members of society, without the economic function, for example the provision and preparation of food, life without cease, and without education, a term Murdock used for socialization, there would be no culture" (Haralambos and Holborn 396). In addition to that, the present study reaffirms that from the ancient times folktales and storytelling were intertwined with all the four universal functions of the family. Stories at mealtimes and bedtimes had several social, cultural, historical, geographical, and psychological rubrics interwoven into the familial fabric. Hence, folktales are identified as pedagogical tools that begin at home, *Akam*.

Love in the heart among humans or nonhumans gets transferred to love for the environment and world at large. Love is seen as a complementary principle that unites the different elements in nature, human beings, and the environment. The study reveals the interstitial spaces and the temporal aspects of the sacred that allow humans to respect and revere life on this planet.

Women represent the nurturing principles of Gaia in classical Tamil poetry. Foster-mothers have a special role in the lives of the heroine in *Akam* poetry. "There are mothers (and foster-mothers) too who go themselves in search of their daughters (gone on elopement with their lovers) along the streets of well-guarded towns and through arid desert-like tracts" (Murugan 386). Poem 378 by Kayamanar from the *Palai* landscape depicts the foster-mother's love for the heroine. The heroine has eloped with the hero and the foster-mother is concerned about her daughter. The poem is in the form of a prayer and a blessing, "Let no sun burn/ may trees shade the little ways on the hill/may the paths be covered with sand/ may cool rain/cool the desert sands/ for that simple girl/ her face the color of the new mango leaf/ who left us/for a man/with the long bright spear" (Murugan 386). Motherhood is seen as an intrinsic quality in all human beings. The spirit of mothering, care, and nurture are central to the folktales as Gaia Care Narratives.

Human life is characterized by cord, discord, and concord. The two major types of love in separation recorded in *Akam* poetry are "the hero parting from the heroine on his male quest and the hero and heroine going on elopement" (Murugan 378). The *Kurinci* Poem 38 is a poem of love in separation which represents the young woman's perception of the environment in relation to her home. It is a poem by Kapilar that defines true love with these words, "His kind of love is good enough/my friend, /for someone strong enough to bear it, /without thinking, /when their eyes are eaten away/by endless tears, /when he is gone" (Balakrishnan 51). The human separation from nature can be seen akin to the separation of the hero and the heroine. The rift between culture and nature in the contemporary scenario can be understood as a phase of separation, pining, and sulking of the lovers in distress. Drawing a leaf out of *Akam* poetry ecofemiotics promises hope and the reunion of humans with nature seen akin to the regeneration of human-nature relationships in the future.

The study underscores a pertinent idea that *akam* poetry is not just a classical literature with aesthetic values, but they are a potential repertoire of an ancient culture to understand the worldviews and consciousness of the people who lived close to nature. The identification of *Akam* concepts in folktales accentuates the interconnectedness and symbiotic nature of life and confirms the value of interdependence and peaceful coexistence. The natural signs and symbols in folktales affirm the relationship among nature, human, and the sacred. The folktales represent human-nature proximity at different levels quite specifically drawing the connection between the mindscape and the landscape, the *topos* and the *oikos*, and promote a culture integrated with nature.

Love begins at home, in *Akam*, and gets translated into care, concern, and benevolence in *Puram*. The love gets transformed into courage and compassion in the world at large. Kaniyan Punkunran's poem 192 of Purananuru has the following lines:

Every town our home town, /Every man a kinsman/Good and evil do not come/from others. /Pain and relief of pain/come of themselves. /Dying is nothing new. /We do not rejoice /That life is sweet/nor in anger/Call it bitter/Our lives, however dear, /Follow their own course. /rafts drifting/

in the rapids of a great river/sounding and dashing over the rocks/after a downpour/from skies slashed by lightnings-/we know this/from the vision/ of men who see. /So, /we are not amazed by the great, /And we do not scorn the little.

(1–24)

The poem connotes Earth as one family where all human beings are relatives. The poem also highlights themes of interconnectedness, interdependence, intrinsic value, and cyclical pattern of life. Similarly, poem 182 by Ilam Peruvaluti goes,

This world lives/because/some men/do not eat alone, /not even when they get/the sweet ambrosia of the gods;/they've no anger in them/they fear evils other men fear/ but never sleep over them/give their lives for honour, / will not touch a gift of whole worlds/if tainted;/there's no faintness in their hearts/and they do not strive/for themselves. /Because such men are, /This world is.

(1–17)

The poems highlight the ethos of the ancient people characterized by abundance, interconnectedness, interdependence, and inherent worth of life.

Human perception of the environment is always seen in relation to her/his home and the "exterior" world. The concerns of *Akam* and *Puram* are understood in unison by both men and women to fulfill the needs and rights of all life forms on this planet. Ideally speaking, *Akam* and *Puram*, Nature and Culture must integrate into an organic whole representing the interconnections among heart, home, and the world. By enabling a holistic approach to analysis, this research accentuates the significance of folktales as environmental discourse, to understand the worldviews and consciousness of the apparently silent and silenced people and envisions authentic expressions of "Nature-Culture". By transcending the polemics of space and time, nature and culture, spirit and matter this study provides a viable space for recognizing ecological voices and their concerns in folktales across the world. Therefore, *Akam* is identified as a congruent philosophy of eco-critical thought as the core ideas, beliefs, and practices are shaped by the harmonious natural principles that govern life on this planet.

Care as a Unifying Principle

Care and compassion are at the center of this eco-critical study. In an old Cherokee Indian tale when a small child asked his grandfather about the battle that goes on in the minds and hearts of people, the storyteller noted that there were two wolves inside of us all, one is evil that includes anger, envy, jealousy, greed, superiority, ego, etc. and the other is good which includes love, hope, peace, joy, humility, benevolence, empathy, generosity, compassion, and truth. When the grandson asked "Which wolf wins?" The old Cherokee simply replied, "The one you feed" (The Tale of Two Wolves). The human mind, heart, and soul have a great impact on their environment. Their thoughts are converted into action every second. They can shape and reshape their environment based on the wolf they feed. The Cherokee tale is about the heart, mind, and the soul which is *Akam*.

Folktale as environmental discourse provides a wide range of possibilities to understand what Cheryll Glotfelty defines in *The Ecocriticism Reader*, "the study of the relation between literature and the physical environment" (xviii). Deep Ecology and Ecofeminism are two main branches of eco-critical thought. Deep Ecology is a movement initiated by Norwegian philosopher Arne Næss in 1972 which posits two main ideas. The first is that there must be a shift away from human-centered anthropocentrism to ecocentrism in which every living thing is seen as having inherent value regardless of its utility. Second, that humans are part of nature rather than superior and apart from it and therefore must protect all life on Earth as they would protect their family or self (Spanne). Folktales in eco-pedagogy validate ecocentrism as a fundamental premise. Humans are part of nature, and they coexist with other forms of life.

Human awareness of Earth-centered time and space is the need of the hour. Deep ecological awareness helps us to understand that life is interconnected and interdependent and is rooted in the cyclical patterns of nature. As Capra and Luisi note,

> Ultimately, deep ecological awareness is spiritual awareness. When the concept of the human spirit is understood as the mode of consciousness in which the individual feels a sense of belonging, of connectedness, to the cosmos as a whole, it becomes clear that ecological awareness is spiritual in its deepest essence.
>
> (13)

The study initiates a process of eco-spiritual understanding that brings together a wide gamut of narratives that promote the wellbeing of life on this planet. "Etymologically", the word "ecosophy" combines oikos and Sophia, "household" and "wisdom" (Naess *Ecology, Community and Lifestyle* 37).

Deep Ecologists Arne Naess and George Sessions conceived the eight principles and along with sociologist Bill Devall documented in the book *Deep Ecology: Living as If Nature Mattered.*

• The well-being and flourishing of human and nonhuman life on Earth have value in themselves (synonyms: inherent worth, intrinsic value, inherent value). These values are independent of the usefulness of the nonhuman world for human purposes.

- Richness and diversity of life forms contribute to the realization of these values and are also values in themselves.
- Humans have no right to reduce this richness and diversity except to satisfy vital needs.
- Present human interference with the nonhuman world is excessive, and the situation is rapidly worsening.
- The flourishing of human life and cultures is compatible with a substantial decrease in the human population. The flourishing of nonhuman life requires such a decrease.
- Policies must therefore be changed. The changes in policies affect basic economic, technological, and ideological structures. The resulting state of affairs will be deeply different from the present.
- The ideological change is mainly that of appreciating life quality (dwelling in situations of inherent worth) rather than adhering to an increasingly higher standard of living. There will be a profound awareness of the difference between big and great.
- Those who subscribe to the foregoing points have an obligation directly or indirectly to participate in the attempt to implement the necessary changes.

(Spanne)

How do folktales signify intrinsic value and interdependence of life? How do these earth-centered narratives promote diversity and pluralistic outlook? How do the folktales emerge as environmental discourse in shaping the policies of environmental sustainability and peaceful coexistence? The study attempts to throw light upon these pertinent concerns. Arne Naess was inspired by the Gandhian ideals of nonviolence and the Buddhist philosophies. The *Akam* earth-centric concept of *Karu* finds resonance in the cardinal principles of Deep Ecology. The respect for intrinsic value is at the core of *Akam* poetics, Anishinaabe beliefs, Aboriginal philosophies, *Adivasi* practices, and Zen way of life.

Ecofemiotics attempts to explore folktales as Gaia Care Narratives to inspire what Stephen Harding calls the "Gaian awareness" (41) through the "four cardinal points of Jung's mandala of the psyche" (41) namely intuition, sensing, feeling, and thinking. The eco-critical understanding of Gaia as a living being is a central metaphor of the study. Once upon a time Gaia, the Earth Mother is supposed to have emanated into existence. Deriving energy from the sun, she gained prominence as an organic living being in the cosmos. She was filled with different life forms nourishing her children who in turn nourished her. Humans were one of them. Humans were endowed with a special gift of storytelling. Through storytelling they were able to emanate positive energy to the environment around them. In the Cree "Grandmother's Creation Story" by Victoria Whitewolf and the Bhil folktale "First There Was Woman" and many other creation myths across the world, the creator made oceans, mountains, plains, lakes, rivers, deserts, animals, birds, and fish before humans, and they lived in balance and harmony. Folktales are socio-cultural expressions of humans rooted in nature. Folktales include myths, legends, fables, parables, fairy tales, tall tales, and anecdotes. The study promotes storytelling as an eco-pedagogical tool to explore ways to reiterate the human responsibility toward Gaia and to reconnect with our Home, our planet Earth.

Remarkably, Four Arrows (Wahinkpe Topa), aka Dr. Don Trent Jacobs a professor in indigenous spirituality, in his famous chart on dominant and indigenous worldview manifestations distinguishes 40 dimensions that promote respect to different cultures, philosophies, religions, and spiritual traditions across the world. Some of the dimensions include: hierarchy and nonhierarchical patterns, fear and courage, self and community, rigidity and fluidity, materialistic and nonmaterialistic outlook, earth as matter and life, the connection between heart and head, an empathetic outlook, anthropocentric and biocentric perspectives, words as sacred with an emphasis on truthfulness, multifaceted approach to truth, attempt to question fragmented systems, belief in spiritual energies and alternative consciousness, time as linear and cyclical, belief in complementary principles, nature as benevolent, nonlinear and linear thinking, and high respect for women (Four Arrows).

The proposed ecofemiotic study believes in love in terms of Jung's emphasis on intuition, sensing, feeling, and thinking as the ubiquitous phenomenon that shapes the minds and tempers the hearts of storytellers and listeners as eco-sensitive learners to work toward a sustainable future. It draws inspiration from Paulo Freire's dialogic pedagogy and his authentic words,

> Dialogue cannot exist, however, in the absence of a profound love for the world and for people. The naming of the world, which is an act of creation and re-creation, is not possible if it is not infused with love. Love is at the same time the foundation of dialogue and dialogue itself . . . No matter where the oppressed are found, the act of love is commitment to their cause – the cause of liberation.
>
> (89)

The love in *Akam* poetry serves as a starting point to envision the universal love for all beings on this planet. As Freire elaborates,

> as an act of bravery, love cannot be sentimental; as an act of freedom, it must not serve as a pretext for manipulation. It must generate other acts of freedom; otherwise, it is not love. Only by abolishing the situation of oppression is it possible to restore the love which that situation made impossible. If I do not love the world – if I do not love life -If I do not love people -I cannot enter into dialogue" (90). Paulo Freire further explains that dialogue "cannot exist without humility".
>
> (90)

It requires "an intense faith . . . in their power to make and remake, to create and re-create faith in the vocation to be more fully human (which is not the privilege of an elite, but the birth right of all)" (90). The eco-pedagogical process promotes faith, humility, care, and love among the learners as a prototype that inspires an alternative socio-economic order characterized by sustainable living, ecological balance, and gender equity.

In order to tackle the man-made issues that have created havoc in this green planet, the study of space-time proximity, nature-culture connection, and spirit-matter relationship in the Gaia Care Narratives through ecofemiotics provide us the opportunity to reforest the planet through an environmental pedagogy where consciousness-raising thoughts and beliefs nurtured by love get converted into transformative reflection and action. An injury to one life on earth has repercussions on all life forms on this planet. The cruelty and exploitation of innocent children, women, men, animals, birds, trees, and land results in the suffering of all life forms across the world. If the word "culture" denotes "respect", then it certainly calls for the reverence of living beings regardless of color, caste, race, or class. Hence, it is important to create, procreate, and recreate narratives of life affirmation to be conscientiously nurtured with care through eco-pedagogy for the well-being of this green planet.

Folktales aim at reweaving the space-time relationship. Returning to the basics and revaluing the motifs and patterns on the intrinsic worth is a way of re-joining sacredness of life. In terms of space-time, it reawakens the consciousness of the parts of the whole and renews the different components of the Earth family. By remodeling and integrating the alternative worldviews Gaia Care Narratives helps us to restructure deep networks. The identification of Gaia Care Narratives attempts to create avenues toward an alternative socio-economic order characterized by love, parity, and justice.

The Marriage of Science and Spirituality

World-renowned environmental philosopher and activist Fritjof Capra began his career as a physicist. He paved the way toward the integration of western science and eco-spirituality. The Deep Ecologist thinker Fritjof Capra claimed that there are close connections between the principles of physics and those of eastern wisdom and philosophies. On the other hand, physicists like Einstein understood the value of Nature.

> I like to experience the universe as one harmonious whole. Every cell has life. Matter, too, has life; it is energy solidified. The tree outside is life . . . The whole of nature is life . . . The basic laws of the universe are simple, but because our senses are limited, we can't grasp them. There is a pattern in creation.
>
> (Web)

Ecofemiotics attempts to map the earth-centered motifs and patterns that radically shape our environmental imagination.

Fritjof Capra's theory on the relationship of western physics and eastern mysticism explains the relation between physics, metaphysics, and the universe. *The Dance of Shiva* by Ananda Coomaraswamy that Capra alludes to in his *The Tao of Physics* explains the relation between physics and Indian mysticism. But interestingly, Shiva is also the god who considered one half of himself as *Shakthi*. Like the primordial feminine principle called *Prakriti* and her companion *Purusha*, Shiva and *Shakthi* represent the *Arthanareeshwarar* (*Shiva* and *Shakthi* as one organic being), symbolizing the complementary nature of both genders. The identification of *Akam* as the microcosm of the macrocosm, the sacred in Nature forms a pertinent goal of this eco-critical analysis in this study. The eco-critical understanding of Nature promises a worldview characterized by sensitivity and spirituality that promotes the wellbeing of life on this Earth. "Our ecology should be a deep ecology – not only deep, but universal" says Thich Nhat Hanh (Hanh 165). The eco-pedagogical framework and the identification of folktales as Gaia Care Narratives unravel the systemic problems and concerns that affect humans and nature alike and recreate an alternative path toward a better socio-economic order characterized by love, parity, and justice.

Lawrence Buell in his work, *The Environmental Imagination* states that "an environmentally oriented work" (7) is characterized by the following aspects:

1. The nonhuman environment is present not merely as a framing device but as a presence that begins to suggest that human history is implicated in natural history.
2. The human interest is not understood to be the only legitimate interest.
3. Human accountability to the environment is part of the text's ethical orientation.
4. Some sense of the environment as a process rather than as a constant or a given is at least implicit in the text.

(7–8)

Folktales emerge as environmentally oriented works as the nonhuman environment is part and parcel of the eco-conscious narrative. The nonhuman beings as an agency are at the center of these narratives shaping human history in relation to natural history. In these earth-centered tales' human interest is tied up with the interest of nonhuman beings and the environment. The stories emanate human stewardship and responsibility toward the wellbeing of the planet. Folktales represent the environment as a process and a continuum and tools of transformation and regeneration.

Types of Akam

Gaia Care Narratives gain sustenance from the rich cornucopia of folktales available across different cultures of the world. Drawing inspiration from the classical, indigenous, and the contemporary eco-critical philosophies Gaia Care Narratives may represent eight types of *Akam* in this study. They are (i) Celebrative *Akam*, (ii) Divisive *Akam*, (iii) Passive *Akam*, (iv) Oppressive *Akam*, (v) Interactive *Akam*, (vi) Collaborative *Akam*, (vii) Transformative *Akam*, and (viii) Regenerative *Akam*.

The celebrative *akam* represents the Edenic world characterized by harmony and peace. It is inspired by love in union and is characterized by interconnectedness, interdependence, and intrinsic value of life. The divisive *akam* shows the disruptions, fragmentations, and reductionism at social, cultural, and environmental levels. The passive *akam* deals with the silent and the silenced down the ages and across the cultures drawing parallels with the agony of love in separation in *akam* poetry. The oppressive *akam* gives an account of the human and nonhuman living beings suppressed and exploited by dominant systems in our society and culture also indicating the pain and suffering that leads to forms of oppression. Interactive *akam* throws light upon the human-nature interaction that is required to bring about a balance characterized by interconnections. Collaborative *akam* tries to connect the dots of benevolence and hope and provides systemic solutions to the systemic problems that create ecological and economic chaos in the contemporary world. Transformative *akam* inspires individual as well as collective change. Regenerative *akam* provides the necessary impetus to bring about social and ecological change.

Earth-centered folktales often begin with the celebrative *akam*. The *akam* denotes a harmonious time-space for humans and all forms of life around them. The Edenic phase represents a high level of spatio-temporal relativity, nature-cultural density, spirituo-physical gravity, and socio-economic parity. However, the harmonious *akam* can also represent the silent and the silenced living beings, nature, women, or other marginalized groups that are passive. For example, in the Kannada folktale "A Flowering Tree" translated by AK Ramanujan, the woman gets transformed into a tree in her mother's house.

> Sister, I'll sit under this tree and meditate. Then you pour the water from this pitcher all over my body. I'll turn into a flowering tree. Then you pluck as many flowers as you want, but do it without breaking a sprout or tearing a leaf. When you're done, pour the water from the other pitcher over me, and I'll become a person again. The younger sister sat down and thought of the Lord. The older one poured water from the first pitcher all over her sister.
>
> (Ramanujan 54)

It is a moment of celebration as she is safe and secure in the environment. In the same way the tree is also safe as the people around respect the sacredness and intrinsic value of life. In contrast to it there are a number of folktales across cultures that drive home themes of incest and silent suffering of women and other marginalized groups and exploitation of nature in a subtle manner. In fairy tales such as Cinderella, Snow White, and Rapunzel the stories begin with a celebrative *akam* when the parents take care of the children with the inherent qualities of nurture that arises from Gaia. Cinderella, Snow White, and Rapunzel depict the oppressive *akam* undergone in different ways. The study attempts to explore not only the oppressive *akam* of the heroines but also the oppressor's *akam*. The stepmother and the stepsisters in Cinderella, the cruel queen in Snow White, and the witch in Rapunzel also experience an oppressive *akam* due to various reasons. Nature acts as an agency in the folktales in the interactive or collaborative *akam*. The interaction between nature and humans provides systemic solutions to the systemic problems that exist in our society. Interaction and collaboration with nature results in transformation and regeneration and in turn social and economic emergence/transformation and nature's regeneration.

The following chapter deals with the development of the integrated ecofemiotic framework that helps us to identify folktales as Gaia Care Narratives.

2 Mindscape, Storyscape, and Signscape

Ecofemiotics

The chapter deals with the development of the *Akam*-inspired ecofemiotic framework to identify and examine folktales as environmental narratives or Gaia Care Narratives that interconnect mindscape with the storyscape and consequently with the signscape. The signs and symbols in the mindscape of the storytellers signify parts that suggest the whole. The mindscape influences the landscape and the landscape influences the mindscape. When nature is embedded in culture, the culture is marked by abundance, interconnectedness, and interdependence of life forms.

In a nutshell, the proposed ecofemiotic framework finds inspiration from systems thinking in theory and practice by connecting the dots among classical philosophies, indigenous beliefs, eco-spiritual traditions, and contemporary eco-critical theories. The characteristics of systems thinking that are in unison with the proposed model are as follows: shift of perspective from the parts to the whole; inherent multidisciplinarity; from objects to relationships; from measuring to mapping; from quantities to qualities; from structures to processes; from objective to epistemic science; and from Cartesian certainty to approximate knowledge (Capra and Luisi 80–82). The study attempts to unite science with spirituality with a purpose to rebuild a world of wellbeing and peaceful coexistence.

As a result, folktales as Gaia Care Narratives offer a systemic space to understand the organic connection between space and time, nature and culture, and spirit and matter contributing to socio-economic balance and order.

The ecofemiotic circumference in Figure. 2.1 represents three pertinent dimensions of environmental humanities in the folktales. They are: (1) Spatio-Temporal Relativity, (2) Naturo-Cultural Density, and (3) Spirituo-Physical Gravity. The following section deals with the origin, evolution, and integration of the ecofemiotic framework that lends itself to the identification of folktales as Gaia Care Narratives.

DOI: 10.4324/9781003406686-3

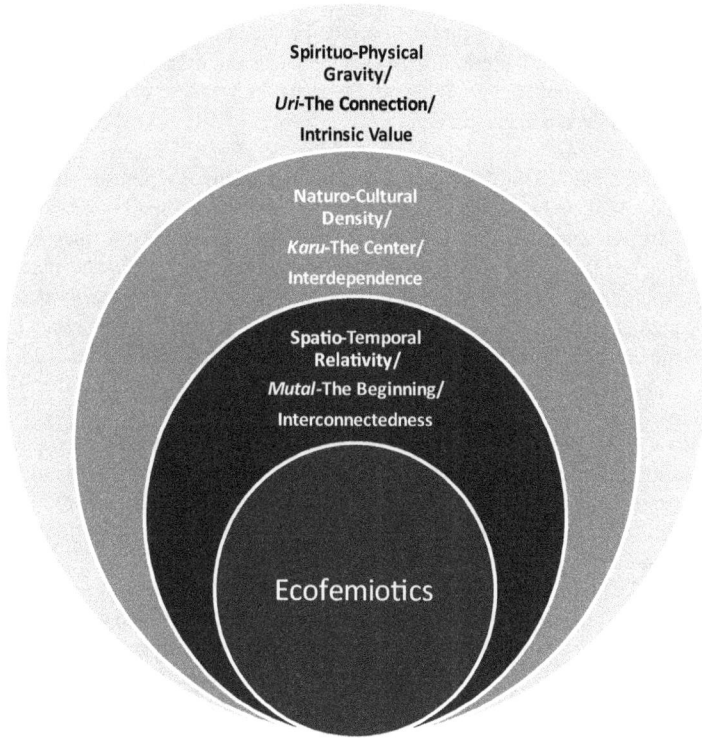

Figure 2.1 The ecofemiotic framework visualized by the author in this study

Spatio-Temporal Relativity

The first dimension of the ecofemiotic framework that helps us to revisit Gaia Care Narratives and realign us with Earth's space-time is called Spatio-Temporal Relativity. In *Akam* poetics, *Mutarporul* is defined as "aspects of land and time, so do men of discernment find" (Murugan 374). By revisiting folktales as earth-centered discourse it is possible to distinguish human and nonhuman aspects of space and time. Human understanding of space-time is related to their mechanistic outlook. Hence it is important to identify the events in a continuum. The relationship between the event and the continuum is nothing but the Zen belief in seeing "eternity in the present moment" (Thich Nhat Hanh 13). The spatio-temporal relativity is characterized by interconnectedness and circular principles of life.

Historically speaking, women's space-time was cyclical in nature whereas men's space-time formed a linear pattern. The life of women in the household/*Akam* was organized in a circular pattern. Women's stories also followed a circular pattern. The hero/heroine sets out on a quest and returns home at the end of the tale. Whereas, the men who went out into the world of *Puram* followed a linear pattern.

In "Women's Time" Kristeva borrows James Joyce's phrase, "father's time, mother's species" to designate two dimensions that human beings have occupied. "Father's Time" refers to the linear time that men have inhabited with the sense of history, destiny and progress. The phrase "mother's species" evokes the realm that women have traditionally occupied: a space that generates the human species, a space like the *chora* on the one hand and a sense of the eternity of the species on the other.

(McAfee 94)

Chora is a term used by Plato in his work *Timaeus* that describes a space where the universe has come to reside. It is a space-time which cannot be destroyed. By revisiting and re-reading the strengths of *Akam* or women's space it is possible to advocate the circular principles as sustainable solutions in the areas of culture, society, and economy.

Spatio-Temporal Relativity consists of three components: space, time-seasons and relativity. The word "relativity", in Tamil deals with connections or attachments. Albert Einstein's theory of relativity deals with the fundamental concepts of space, time, matter, energy, and gravity. Spatio-Temporal Relativity examines the first (*Akam* concept of *Mutal* meaning "first" or "beginning") organic connection between space and time characterized by interconnectedness and circular pattern of life in the folktales. Rachel Carson begins her magnum opus *Silent Spring* with the following words:

The history of life on earth has been a history of interaction between living things and their surroundings. To a large extent, the physical form and the habits of the earth's vegetation and its animal life have been molded by the environment. Considering the whole span of earthly time, the opposite effect, in which life actually modifies its surroundings, has been relatively slight. Only within the moment of time represented by the present century has one species – man – acquired significant power to alter the nature of his world.

(5)

Human beings are complex living creatures who try to comprehend the world through time and space. Apart from the earthly time, the human interpretation of time depends upon their observations and experiences. Depending upon sunrise and sunset they defined day, night, dawn, and dusk. According to Tolkaapiyam, "*Mutarporul* is Aspects of land and time" (Murugan 374) understood by human beings. As Fritjof Capra explains, "relativity theory has thus shown that all measurements involving space and time lose their absolute significance and forced us to abandon the classical concepts of an absolute space and an absolute time" (*The Tao of Physics* 183). Furthermore, Capra elaborates, "throughout eastern mysticism there seems to be a strong intuition for the 'space-time' character of reality. The fact that space and time are inseparably linked, which is so characteristic of relativistic physics, is stressed again and again" (*The Tao of Physics* 189). As energy is central to Einstein's theory of Relativity, *Shakthi* the all-pervading cosmic principle unites the other aspects of this poetic relativity.

In contrast to the modern era, humans who lived during the pre-patriarchal, pre-industrial times believed in a holistic view of life. As GN Devy explains,

> They accept a worldview in which nature, man and God are intimately linked, and they believe in the human ability to spell and interpret truth. They live more by intuition than by reason, they consider the space around them more sacred than secular, and their sense of time is personal rather than objective. The world of the tribal imagination, therefore, is radically different from that of modern Indian society.
>
> (x)

Devy further explains, "the tribal mind has a more acute sense of time than sense of space. Somewhere along the history of human civilization, tribal communities seem to have realized that domination over territorial space was not their lot" (xi). Similar to indigenous concepts, Ecofemiotics attempts to challenge human-centric space-time and promote Earth-centric space-time.

In the dominant mainstream mechanistic worldview, the human interpretation of space-time is linear, reductionist, mechanistic, and fragmented. As Stephan Harding put it,

> There has always been a holistic, integrative strand in western culture, espousing an animistic understanding, that ran alongside the reductionist scientific mainstream. One can even make a good case that the integrative and reductionist modes of consciousness are both innate to the human organism, and that they have manifested in different cultures in different ways in different times.
>
> (29)

By revisualizing space-time in folktales, it is possible to realign animistic space and time according to the principles of Gaia which forms a significant goal of this study. According to the Zen philosophies love is without boundaries, beyond space and time. They are characterized by four dimensions namely: *maitri*, "loving kindness, friendship or companionship" (Thich Nhat Hanh 233); *karuna*, "compassion that heals" (Thich Nhat Hanh 233); *mudita*, "true love that brings joy" (Thich Nhat Hanh 234); and *upeksa*, "inclusivity" (meaning of no-self) (Thich Nhat Hanh 234) which characterize Earth-centric space-time. Space and time in folktales follow circular motifs and patterns that represent a holistic outlook of life. For example, the Indian folk song goes,

> We offer flowers to you,/O doorstep of the house, be kind/Fill the granary with corn./It is the festival of flowers/We offer flowers to you,/O threshold of the house!/May God bless you with an auspicious new year./May your granary fill till it overflows,/May your crops thrive and wealth grow./Let these seasons and months come again./If we survive our times/the Phool Sankranti will return.
>
> (1–12)

By redialing the circular patterns, the folklore emerges as counter-narratives for the wellbeing of life.

Folktales as Gaia Care Narratives initiate the process of reconnecting nature with culture. It involves the quintessential pedagogical process of redeeming and mapping nature's patterns for a better future. Environmental movements across the world such as the Chipko movement against deforestation and Green Belt Movement for afforestation abound with life-affirming narratives that can emerge as Gaia Care Narratives. By reaffirming the proximity of nature-culture it is possible to create two significant processes namely: revisiting the culture of the natural world and redefining the culture centered on nature. These twin goals are augmented by identifying the signs and symbols, motifs, and patterns that represent greater nature-cultural density and value characterized by human love for nature and Gaia's love for all her children.

Looking at earth-based Gaian patterns and motifs in a conscious mindful manner is the need of the hour. Drawing inspiration from nature, the study believes in the importance of reconstructing Earth designs in different areas of life. For example, the five types of landscapes in the *Akam* poetry are *Kurinci* (mountains), *Mullai* (forests), *Marutam* (farmlands), *Neytal* (coastal area), and *Palai* (wasteland). The mountains signify sublimity, the forests symbolize abundance, the farmlands indicate benevolence, the coastal plains suggest hope, and the arid land signifies regeneration. In *Akam* poetry, the fauna, flora, and the lifeworld are seen as an organic process rather than a structure that is called *Karu* which means "embryo in the womb". Why did the ancient Tamil poetics Tolkaapiyam place nature as *Karu* in *Akam* poetry and not *Puram* poetry? The thrust upon nature-centeredness in the interior world, in the mind, heart, and soul would have an unequivocal bearing on the exterior world. This pertinent idea sums up the philosophy of Gaia Care Narratives. Hence, by reassessing nature-centrism it is possible to regenerate an earth-centric lifeworld.

Folktales have a circular narrative pattern. In terms of space and time Gaia Care Narratives promote the significance of circular patterns in understanding the nonhuman world. Mother Earth's love for her children is found in the seasonal changes and the temporal patterns in nature. "Botany in the Rainforest" is a short folktale by Liza Hobbs written in the form of a poem.

> First, the nurse tree must die
> It must fall
> no matter slow or fast
> it must let go of sky,
> lie forever lengthwise
> in deadly moist embrace.

It must rot.

> . . .
> It's straightline nurselings
> Will confound the innocent:
> "What planted such a row
> In these chaotic woodlands?"
> There will be no trace.
> After the final consummation,
> The line of new trees will remain.
> But first, and long before, the nurse must die.
>   (1–7, 10–17)

The poem indicates the cyclical pattern of nature in the forests. When humans live in close proximity with nature, they do not break this cycle. When humans do not understand the inherent spatio-temporal relativity of the forests, the nature-cultural density of flora, fauna, and the lifeworld, and the spirituo-physical gravity of life forms, they disrupt the harmonious life processes. The story emphasizes the sacrifice and selflessness of the "nurse tree" to create a new forest and hence exemplifies a regenerative *akam*. These stories help us to revisit culture on nature and redefine nature of culture.

Stories represent a microcosm. They exist in a space-time continuum. Folktales provide us an opportunity to interrogate the mechanistic understanding of space-time in contrast to the space-time consciousness of nonhuman life. In the indigenous and folk narratives, land, water, the elements, the sun, the moon, and the stars are beyond human space-time. However, they follow a natural rhythm and pattern of their own. Folktales can help humans to mimic these patterns to promote love and care for the well-being of the planet. Folktales emerge as environmental signs that reshape the imagination of humans to work toward a better society that is characterized by sustainability and balance.

Naturo-Cultural Density

"Nature and Culture, or rather nature and culture, are inseparable. Thinking about the nature of natures, the culture of cultures, the nature of cultures, and the culture of natures is a natural impulse for humans" (Steiner 8). Naturo-Cultural Density underscores the symbiotic relation between nature and culture in terms of interdependence and is studied in the folktales as Gaia Care Narratives. The flora, fauna, and humans exist as inter-beings and signify the embryo in the womb of Gaia/Mother Earth. Naturo-Cultural Density is the second dimension of the ecofemiotic framework that consists of three aspects: nature, culture, sign, and density. Density is the mass of a unit volume of a material substance.

> Nature can mean something that is essential to a person or a thing . . .
> By the nineteenth century, the dominant meaning of 'nature' had changed
> again. This time it was seen as a whole material world of things rather than
> a series of forces.
>
> (Giddens Anthony and Philips W. Sutton 156)

The density of the conscious word of the storyteller/narrator challenges the materialistic worldview and promotes a biocentric worldview through folktales as Gaia Care Narratives.

Naturo-Cultural Density underscores the symbiotic relation between nature and culture in terms of interdependence and is studied in the folktales as Gaia Care Narratives. The five types of landscape indicate the intricate connection between the nature, culture, and the sacred in the lines, and the hilly tract, *Kurinci*; the forest tract, *Mullai*; the cultivable tract, *Marutam*; the littoral tract, *Neytal*; and the Arid tract, *Palai* represent diversity and abundance of Mother Nature. The Naturo-Cultural Density is the second dimension of the framework that consists of three aspects: nature, culture, and density. Density is the mass of a unit volume of a material substance. The density of the conscious word of the storyteller/narrator that cares for the environment contributes to Gaia Care Narratives.

Akam poetics reveals that the people who live close to nature believe that natural environment and the nonhuman beings around us are like the embryo in the womb that needs to be nurtured and protected with care. The word "culture" is often used in contrast to nature. "The things that humans produce or do are cultural, whereas the things that exist or occur without human intervention are part of the natural environment" (Haralambos and Holborn 727). Flora, fauna, and the lifeworld are organically connected through the naturo-cultural density in the *Akam* tradition. For example, "The Unicorn Song", an Irish traditional folk song written down by children's author Shel Silverstein and popularized by the Canadian band Irish Rovers in the 1960s, goes:

> A long time ago, when the Earth was green/There were more kinds of
> animals than you've ever seen/They'd run around free while the Earth

was being born/And the loveliest of all was the unicorn/There were green alligators and long-necked geese/Some humpty backed camels and some chimpanzees/Some cats and rats and elephants, but sure as you're born/ The loveliest of all was the unicorn.

(1–8)

The flora and fauna were a part of this planet even before the advent of humans. The folk song reiterates the nature-cultural density of the folk text in representing interdependence of life forms on this Earth.

Through an ecofemiotic re-reading, folktales as Gaia Care Narratives try to bridge nature and culture where stories also become "interbeings". It attempts to find earth-centered motifs and patterns that are already a part of the cultural process of the human beings who are narrating the tale, listening to the tale, reading a tale, or writing a tale, and as a result as Thich Nhat Hanh puts it, "the insight of interbeing has the power to wake us up" (2). When humans understand the "inter-be" connection with the subjects of nature, they contribute to the mindful ways of understanding Gaia Care Narratives. "When we try to pick out anything by itself", said John Muir, "we find it hitched to everything else in the universe" (Ingram et al. 11). This spirit of interconnectedness among human and nonhuman beings inspires us to revisit and revive indigenous stories as Gaia Care Narratives.

Akam believes in a holistic outlook and cyclical pattern of life. Respect for the intrinsic value of life is one of the fundamental premises in this culture integrated with nature. According to Tolkappiyam, there are single-sense organisms which have the sense of touch; two-sense organisms have the sense of touch and taste; three-sense organisms have the sense of touch, taste, and smell; four-sense organisms have sight, touch, taste, and smell; five sense organisms have hearing in addition; and the mind's faculty is the sixth sense, according to the discerning humans (Murugan 630). Hence, the intrinsic value of each and every life form is fundamental to *Akam* theory and forms the basis of ecofemiotics.

"I Will Be a Hummingbird" is an ecological tale narrated by Wangari Maathai, the founder of Green Belt Movement. During a forest fire all the animals are in despair. They run out of the woods and watch the fire engulfing the forest. The little hummingbird represents Gaia and her love for all her children. She tries to put out the fire by carrying water droplets in her tiny beak. Wangari Maathai visualizes herself as the hummingbird trying to save the planet from destruction. In terms of the spatio-temporal relativity the event of forest fire contributes to the awakening of human responsibility in the continuum. The relationship among the birds and animals, trees, and plants are marked by interconnectedness. The hummingbird takes an extraordinary effort to respect the sacredness of the forests and all life forms. Thus, Wangari Maathai's story inspires the readers and the listeners to reinvent the mindscape according to the environmental needs for a transformative and regenerative *akam*. The forest symbolizes a microcosm marked by diversity and pluralistic outlook. Like the hummingbird, the bees, butterflies, and bats as keystone species contribute their might to earth's continuum and existence. The hummingbird signifies the worldview of abundance. This Gaia Care Narrative helps us to understand the transformative *akam* and regenerative *akam* to redeem nature's patterns and reaffirm nature-culture.

Spirituo-Physical Gravity

What connects *Akam* with Zen? It is love and the spirit of abundance that connects spirit with matter. As Thich Nhat Hanh in his book, *Zen and the Art of Saving the Planet* puts it, "if you have the mind of love, you are what can be called a buddha in action" (11). *Akam* in congruence with the ecological Zen-based philosophy attempts to underscore the role of storytellers as buddhas in action. Thich Nhat Hanh poses a clarion call to the human species on our planet.

> The extinction of species is taking place every day. Researchers estimate that every year over twenty thousand species go extinct, and the rate is accelerating. This is what is happening now; it's not something in the future. We know that 251 million years ago there was already global warming caused by gigantic volcanic eruptions, and the warming caused the worst mass extinction in our planet's history. The six-degree Celsius increase in global temperature was enough to wipe out 95 percent of the species that were alive. Now a second massive warming is taking place. This time there is also manmade deforestation and industrial pollution. Perhaps within a hundred years there may be no more humans on the planet. After the last mass extinction, it took the Earth 100 million years to restore life. If our civilization disappears, it will take a similar time for another civilization to reappear.
>
> (13)

Through the proposed framework the ecofemiotic study attempts to identify Gaia Care Narratives as environmental discourses that fulfill the human obligation toward Mother Earth, to spread the nature-centric theories of interconnectedness, interdependence, and intrinsic value of life.

"Earth-based spirituality calls us to live with integrity" claims the ecofeminist thinker Starhawk (Diamond and Orenstein 74). Spirituo-Physical Gravity (drawing inspiration from the *Akam* concept of *Uri* meaning the "relationships" or "connection") draws the inherent connection between spirit and matter redefining the nature-nature, human-nature, and human-human relationships in the folktales as Gaia Care Narratives. The fivefold *Akam* love behavior namely "union, separation, endurance, pining and sulking" (Murugan 378) can be interpreted from the point of view of Gaia's relationship with the humans. The word "gravity" denotes the power that makes objects attract toward the earth, and at this point the energy or *Shakthi* that resides at the core of the floral motif aligns with the gravitational pull of the universe reinstating the importance of being simple, down to Earth and the need to go in search of roots. In physics, the center of gravity is an imaginary point in a body of matter where the total weight of the body may be thought to be concentrated. In this study *Shakthi* is identified as the focal point that helps human beings to maintain their equilibrium.

> The concept of Shakthi has a direct bearing on the lives of simple women who strive hard to protect their environment. It is perceived as a dynamic force that guides their minds and motivates their spirits in achieving what they want to achieve.
>
> (Porselvi Nature, Culture and Gender 50)

Furthermore, *Ahimsa* or nonviolence is considered as *Stree Shakthi* in Indian culture that helps a woman maintain her balance and equilibrium.

The respect for the intrinsic value of all life forms and the reverence to sacredness springs from the idea of "interbeing" what Thich Nhat Hanh describes "I inter-am. It is closer to the truth in the light of interconnectedness, interbeing" (19).

> Thay said, "If you are a poet, you will see clearly that there is a cloud floating on this sheet of paper. Without a cloud there is no rain; without the rain, the tree cannot grow; and without trees, we cannot make paper. The cloud is essential for the paper to exist . . . So, we can say that the cloud and the paper inter-are. Realizing and touching the universal truth of what he meant by 'interbeing', our interdependence with all of life and Nature, had expanded my heart space, blossoming beyond compassion to self, to an openness for healing others and the Earth."
>
> (Quach)

It is the opposite of fragmentation and separateness which characterizes the contemporary society. This notion of interbeing is also captured in the African indigenous concept of "Ubuntu". An anthropologist who had been studying the culture of an African tribe put a fruit basket under a tree. He gathered up the children in the village and told them to run a race to get the fruit basket. To his surprise the children took each other's hands and ran together to the tree. Then they sat together around the basket and enjoyed the fruits as a group. The anthropologist was quite shocked and he asked why they all went together when one of them could have won all the fruits for himself/herself? A young child looked up to him and uttered, "How can one of us be happy if all the other ones are sad?" (The Story of Ubuntu). The word *Ubuntu* signifies the interconnectedness, interdependence, and intrinsic value of life that exist or should exist between people as conscious living beings in this planet. It refers to behaving well toward others or acting in ways that are beneficial to the community, the environment, and the society at large. The story confirms the life-affirming view that all the components of the planet are parts of the larger whole, the organic being called Gaia.

Spirituo-Physical Gravity (drawing inspiration from the *Akam* concept of *Uri* meaning the "relationships" or "connection") draws the inherent connection between spirit and matter redefining the nature-nature, human-nature, and human-human relationships in the folktales as Gaia Care Narratives. In physics, the center of gravity is an imaginary point in a body of matter where the total weight of the body may be thought to be concentrated.

Fritjof Capra in his *The Web of Life* explicates the significance of Deep Ecology as a new paradigm for social and environmental change.

Ultimately, deep ecological awareness is spiritual or religious awareness. When the concept of the human spirit is understood as the mode of consciousness in which the individual feels a sense of belonging, of connectedness, to the cosmos as a whole, it becomes clear that ecological awareness is spiritual in its deepest essence. It is, therefore, not surprising that the emerging new vision of reality based on deep ecological awareness is consistent with the so-called "perennial philosophy" of spiritual traditions, whether we talk about the spirituality of Christian mystics, that of Buddhists or the philosophy and cosmology underlying the Native American traditions.

(7)

The respect for the intrinsic value of all life forms and the reverence to sacredness spring from the idea of "interbeing" what Thich Nhat Hanh describes "I inter-am. It is closer to the truth in the light of interconnectedness, interbeing" (19).

The ecofemiotic study enables a conscious recognition of the interconnections between the folktales that emerge as Gaia Care Narratives. For a very long time narratives of hopelessness and despair, pain and suffering, and oppression and anxiety are doing the rounds in the area of environment, society, economy, and health. Revisiting the life-affirming folktales of people who live close to nature is the need of the hour. Love inspires mindful ways of living. The folktales as Gaia Care Narratives motivate the humans to be mindful in their thoughts and conscientious in their action. This results in reacclimatizing wellbeing as the primary purpose of life on this planet.

Stories as life-affirming environmental discourse emerge as social symbols of hope. According to George Herbert Mead,

human thought, experience and conduct are essentially social. They owe their nature to the fact that human beings interact in terms of symbols, the most important of which are contained in language . . . Symbols provide the means whereby humans can interact meaningfully with their natural and social environment. They are human made and refer not to the intrinsic nature of objects and events but to the ways in which people perceive them . . . Without symbols there would be no human interaction and no human society.

(Haralambos and Holborn 978)

Human interaction is symbolic. Folktales represent a symbolic world that represents the earth-centered values and beliefs that promise a sustainable society.

The earth-centered tales attempt to bridge nature and culture where stories also become "interbeings". It attempts to find earth-centered motifs and patterns that are already a part of the cultural process of the human beings who are narrating the tale, listening to the tale, reading a tale or writing a tale and as a result as Thich Nhat Hanh puts it, "the insight of interbeing has the power to wake us up" (2). When humans understand the "inter-be" connection with the subjects of nature, they contribute the mindful ways to Gaia Care Narratives. This spirit of interconnectedness inspires us to revisit and revive indigenous stories as Gaia Care Narratives.

There has always been a holistic understanding of life among the indigenous cultures across the world. The ecofemiotic tool in this study challenges the dominant ideologies of the Anthropocene era that have contributed to the ecological and economic chaos and re-bridge the dichotomies that separate nature from culture, man from woman, self and the other, the mindscape and the landscape, humans and nonhumans, and the home from the outside world. Woman-nature proximity affirms the belief that woman power is nature power and vice versa. It explores the fluidity of nature, culture, gender, and sacred as parts of the larger whole, the *Akilam* (the universe). The transition from the *Akam* to the *Akilam* happens when human beings turn inward and explore the interior, the heart and the home/oikos in relation to the larger home/our cosmos in the *Akaram*. Emerging from the seeds of indigenous nature-centered philosophies the study can be understood as theory and practice that promotes planetary consciousness where Gaia Care Narratives are identified as tools to reengineer the Anthropocene.

The ecofemiotic framework encourages us to identify different types of motifs such as time, seasons, space, elements, directions, land, water, flora, fauna, totem, lifeworld, sacred, love, motherhood, sisterhood, kinship, and sharing. The mapping of these motifs and patterns in cross-cultural indigenous and folk narratives inspires an alternative way of looking at life. The *Akam* ethos of the Tamil *Cankam* period find concurrence with the Anishinaabe traditions and the Aboriginal cultures on the other side of the world. Folktales as Gaia Care Narratives help us to fulfill the human obligation toward Mother Earth and all her Children.

Returning to the roots is reviving our connection with Mother Earth. The Big Thunder speaks of the Earth in the following way.

The Great Spirit is our Father, but the earth is our mother. She nourishes us. What we put in the ground she gives back to us, and healing plants as well. If we are wounded, we go to our mother and seek to lay the wounded part against her, to be healed.

(Zimmerman 89)

Humans have a connection to the soil as the roots of the giant banyan tree, as a child is intrinsically connected to the mother through the umbilical cord. Hence, this study envisions a radical reshaping of the human consciousness for creating alternative networks that work in favor of Gaia/Mother Earth.

Moving beyond analysis this study attempts to synthesize Gaia motifs and patterns into an integrated network. The decoding of earth-centered signs and symbols in folktales is followed by recoding of motifs and patterns in Gaia Care Narratives. The mapping of earth-centered themes and motifs has a bearing on the mind, heart, and the soul of both the storyteller and the listener.

Recreating folktales as Gaia Care Narratives is the need of the hour. In the nature-centric stories land has a voice, water has a voice, birds and animals express concerns, and trees shower their love on the living beings around them. Humans are not at the center of these narratives. Instead, they form a part of the larger web of life. However, the major challenge in re-reading the folktales is countering the anthropocentric viewpoint. Humans have the tendency to attribute qualities to the nonhuman living beings and nonliving things. Why are the foxes considered cunning? Why are the serpents termed evil? Why are the hyenas considered evil and ugly and why are the lions glorified? Gaia Care Narratives attempt to caution the narrators and storytellers to be mindful of anthropocentrism and narrate the story from an earth-centered perspective.

Gaia is the *Shakthi* or the inherent power within all living forms. All living and nonliving forms shape Gaia. Every atom of life contributes to Gaia the living planet. This adds on to the worldview of abundance. The chapter attempts to document the exploration of motifs and patterns that uphold a systems view of life. Gaia is a loving mother who personifies balance. She is characterized by care and regeneration. The ecofemiotic study focuses on the importance of Gaia Care Narratives in shaping the consciousness of humans to work toward sustainable living. By drawing theories from various disciplines such as literature, movements, systems theories, and sociological and economic theories, the study aims at identifying the systemic problems that oppress the planet and all her marginalized children and offer systemic solutions through the earth-centered tales. The major concerns of the study are: to identify motifs and patterns that represent alternative space-time characterized by interconnectedness and circular principles of time; to recognize the significance of green narratives with nature-culture proximity marked by interdependence; to examine Gaia Care Narratives that uphold spirit-matter relationship characterized by intrinsic value or inherent worth; and to study the alternative social-economic order embedded in the green narratives characterized by sustainability and balance.

Gaia Care Narratives include myths, fables, parables, legends, fairy tales, anecdotes, etc. Folk songs, dance, and drama also includes the narrative element which is life-affirming. Lullabies, children's songs, love songs, nuptial songs, and dirge also include stories. Gaia Care Narratives show the interdependent relationship between human beings and the natural environment. In these tales, animals, birds, plants, trees, and other objects in nature are acknowledged, respected, and at times, worshipped, most often by women and children. Each and every living creature in nature has a special role to play in these folktales.

Words, sentences, signs, symbols, and stories are born into this world every second of human life. This act of verbal procreation can be both positive and negative. Positive thoughts deliver positive words which in turn create positive action. On the other hand, negative words lead onto negative action. The indigenous tribes across the world believe that stories are living beings composed of words, symbols, and sounds. In an era of indifference and insensitivity, through ecofemiotics, Gaia Care Narratives are envisioned as conscious visionaries with a vocation to reweave the world. They subvert dominant malevolent discourses of power, suppression, and injustice and rewrite new histories and her-stories to heal our planet.

In the past, very often, the world has witnessed the narratives of the powerful silencing the narratives of the powerless. The stories of the weak, marginalized, and the other are aborted as fetus or smothered in infancy. The muffled voices and the stifled expressions are soon forgotten and lost. Human beings have the right to expression in each and every moment of their lives. For example, in the Indian folktale "A Story and a Song" a woman feels suffocated when she is not able to voice out her stories and songs. Likewise, in "A Story in Search of an Audience" the woman goes in search of a listener to narrate her story. The respect for other beings is shown only through their power of listening. For several centuries, women and other marginalized groups were silent or silenced by the patriarchal society. The binary opposition of nature vs. culture, spirit vs. matter, and man vs. woman in the dominant western ideologies has created a major havoc in the present era. The acknowledgment of the role of women has been minimal in all walks of life, especially in the developing and the underdeveloped countries. The lack of participation of women in shaping the societies and cultures in the recent past has resulted in the ecological chaos, the economic crisis, the political unrest, and the social disintegration. At this juncture, it is important to redefine the role of women and the other marginalized groups as messengers of simplicity, goodwill, peace, and hope in rebuilding the ethos of a new era. Re-reading folktales as Gaia Care Narratives using an ecofemiotic framework is a clarion call to the human race which is in deep slumber.

Stories that promote interconnectedness and interdependence must be set in motion through the identification of Gaia Care Narratives. In the villages when a child falls down and cries, the parent says, "We will hit the earth . . . you don't cry". This simple day-to-day word ritual leaves a permanent mark on the child that if she/he is injured, she/he should punish others around him/her. In contrast, the child must be told that she/he should be careful next time. A child must know that hurting his/her neighbor is like hurting himself/herself or hurting Mother Earth/Gaia. Education of universal wellbeing begins at home. The spirit of nonviolence or *Ahimsa* is an inherent quality in mothers. Through Gaia Care Narratives, men and women can communicate the qualities of motherhood and Mother Earth hood in their thoughts, words, and deeds.

Gaia Care Narratives uphold stories of care and concern for Mother Earth: stories about the protection of trees, mountains, soil, and water; stories of abundance and benevolence; stories of humans gaining strength from the forests and woodlands; stories about simplicity and sensitivity to nonhuman life; stories of regeneration and revival; stories of the sacred and the healing processes; stories of togetherness and peaceful coexistence; stories of the human-nature continuum. Gaia Care Narratives endow a special role and responsibility on the human race to realize their potential as agents of change for the welfare of all life forms.

Folktales are potent seeds that have a healing touch on the teller and the told. Narratives with destructive intent are floated across several modes of communication in this digital era. As a counter-current through eco-Storytelling of Gaia Care Narratives, it is imperative to create positive, constructive, holistic narratives that will nurture hope in the young minds, the flag bearers, and the torch bearers of the future society. Stories of greed, avarice, and discontent must be balanced with stories of benevolence, magnanimity, and contentment. Tales of treachery and narrow-mindedness must be balanced with tales of truth, trust, and abundance. Legends of individual achievements and attainments must be balanced with stories of collective strength.

Storytelling is a Zen method of consciousness-raising in this study. It emphasizes the importance of "now" or the present moment in relation to the past and the future. They underscore the cyclical pattern of life. But unfortunately, the youth of today are unaware of the bigger picture. They are grappling with the bits and pieces of the giant jigsaw puzzle in a hasty manner. Through storytelling one can rekindle the passion to narrate holistic stories of heirloom that are productive to the person and his/her society. Gaia Care Narratives aim at praxis where reflective stories end up as responsible action. On the other hand, the stories that do not inspire people into action can be called dead stories. They do not have life in them. The affirmative Gaia Care Narratives as living seeds are fortified and nurtured by the power of love and care for fellow beings in this planet.

The Covid-19 pandemic is only a symptom, the tip of the iceberg. There are worse, deep-rooted problems in our society and environment. Farmers die of poverty and debts. Women die of harassment, rape, ill health, and domestic violence. Children die of malnutrition and abuse. Migrants die of hunger. The connecting thread that links all these social problems is the mismanagement of fundamental structures controlled by patriarchy, materialism, and a consumerist society. Critically conscious men and women have the responsibility of creating a repertoire of time-tested authentic stories that create alternative avenues through Earth-centered altruistic ideologies that will result in authentic transformative action. And, Gaia Care Narratives are here to pave a way toward sustainable development, gender equity, and social justice.

Akam is what the Zen philosophers believe "the way out is in" (Thich Nhat Hanh 46). Human actions depend upon our thoughts. *Akam* the interior world which signifies the heart, mind, and soul inspires *Puram* the exterior world where reflections get transformed into action. When *Akam* is characterized by love, it complements to the *Puram* characterized by courage, benevolence, and wellbeing. This chapter outlines the central aim of the book, the scope of the study, and the pertinent theories and philosophies that have shaped this framework.

Quintessentially, these earth narratives help us to reconcile with earth spirituality to recreate a culture of love and care. This is done by returning to the basics and rebuilding elements of sacredness in everyday life. By understanding the spirituo-physical gravity in the folktales it is possible to reawaken eco-consciousness among children and youth for a better future. In the process they revalue the intrinsic worth of nonhuman living beings and the environment and renew our earth family with respect, compassion, and stewardship. The following chapter deals with the analysis and synthesis of folktales as Gaia Care Narratives.

3 Folktales as Gaia Care Narratives

Re-Genesis of Gaia

Long long ago, so long ago, Gaia was the name given to the Greek goddess of Earth and the name also signified Earth as a living planet. In his preface to *Gaia: A New Look at Life on Earth* James Lovelock notes that the word "Gaia" came from his good friend William Golding who named the living planet after the Greek goddess of the earth. Gaia is a living whole formed by other living beings as parts of the whole embedded within her. The inter-relationships between the parts of the whole confirm Gaia as a living being. Gaia represents the whole of the parts and humans as parts of the giant organic body that signifies interconnectedness of life.

The study gives an account of an integrative method called ecofemiotics to identify and reforest the spirit of abundance, interconnectedness, interde-pendence, and intrinsic value of life in folktales which is called as Gaia Care Narratives. In this study, Gaia is envisioned as an acronym for "God Aspect in All" that denotes sacredness of all life forms. Gaia signifies a continuum. Love signifies a continuum. Nature signifies a continuum. Earth-centric narra-tives signify a continuum. Events in a continuum due to human interventions that are characterized by mindfulness form a harmonious part of the Earth's continuum. On the other hand, mindless acts of human beings result in events that are characterized by chaos and confusion and provide discordant notes to the wellbeing of the planet. The chapter deals with the analysis of folktales in terms of the three-dimensional *Akam*-inspired ecofemiotic framework.

Gaia Care Narratives are identified as living beings who seek to transform their world around them. As Brenda Beck puts it,

> Folktales and legends have persisted in cultures around the world . . . sometimes for thousands of years. They have a life of their own that can far outlive our own short time on earth. This is not an accident. Folktales and legends (the folktale's longer format) would not endure if they were mere child's play . . . packaged in a verbal format . . . A tale can take on a

DOI: 10.4324/9781003406686-4

life of its own, and so can (and so should) the imagination of the person who is determined to explore it.

(Porselvi *Sylvan Tones* vii)

Stories exist as living beings in our day-to-day lives. The life-affirming earth-centered tales emerge as Gaia Care Narratives promising sustainable living and universal wellbeing. In a world fraught with ecological chaos and economic confusion, reengineering the Anthropocene is visualized as a pertinent goal of the proposed ecological theory. Simplicity is at the core of Gaia Care Narratives. Humans have the tendency to reform themselves according to their environmental needs. Indigenous and classical philosophies concur with contemporary eco-critical theories to form a holistic praxis where humans as conscious benevolent species with love for their environment can find multi-dimensional ways of restructuring the existing systems and re-engineering the Anthropocene. By highlighting the systemic problems created by a mechanistic outlook, it is possible to find alternative ways of restructuring our mind to work toward the wellbeing of our planet Earth.

Humans are endowed with the unique power of storytelling fortified by love that can contribute to the wellbeing of nonhuman life. The Pulitzer Prize winner Edward O. Wilson in his book *Half-Earth: Our Planet's Fight for Life* (2016) begins his prologue with the following lines:

What is man? Storyteller, mythmaker, and destroyer of the living world. Thinking with a gabble of reason, emotion, and religion. Lucky accident of primate evolution during the late Pleistocene. Mind of the biosphere. Magnificent in imaginative power and exploratory drive, yet yearning to be more master than steward of a declining planet. Born with the capacity to survive and evolve forever, able to render the biosphere eternal also. Yet arrogant, reckless, lethally predisposed to favour self, tribe, and short-term futures. Obsequious to imagined higher beings, contemptuous toward lower forms of life.

(1)

The storytellers who live close to nature believe in the sacredness of life. Their worldviews are quite contrary to the dominant worldviews in our societies.

Folktales as Gaia Care Narratives emerge as human offerings to the Earth Mother. "Offering is a gift . . . food is an offering, and a story can be an offering" (Doerfler et.al. xv) according to Margaret Noori. According to Anishinaabe teachers, the arrow is not aimed at prey but is instead a metaphor representing the transfer of information. In its tip are stories, epiphanies, and glimpses of eternity passed from one generation to another. Stories affirm life as a continuum. They are considered as living beings. Gaia Care Narratives are a cultural component of humans that has nature at its center. The significance of the indigenous tales as Gaia Care Narratives is in line with GN Devy's comment,

> Most tribal communities in India are culturally similar to tribal communities elsewhere in the world. They live in groups that are cohesive and organically unified. They show very little interest in accumulating wealth or in using labor as a device to gather interest and capital.
>
> (x)

Hence, folktales emerge as potent Gaia Care Narratives that can reweave an alternative environmental imagination for a sustainable way of life.

Gaia Care Narratives draw inspiration from the earth-centered ideologies and principles from different indigenous and classical spiritual traditions. Through this meaning-making process the study explores the questions such as: What is the significance of Earth-centered Gaia Care Narratives or stories in the contemporary times? How do Gaia Care Narratives help people to find a voice for themselves and for their environment? Where does Gaia Care Narratives begin? And what is the impact of Gaia Care narratives on our society, culture economy, and environment? The word "environment" is defined as "the non-human, natural world within which human societies exist. In its broadest sense, the environment is the planet earth" (Giddens 997). Revisiting the folktales as tools of social and environmental change is the need of the hour. The storytelling process initiates a quest for eco-cognition involving human thought processes of perception, understanding, and interpretation.

Space-Time Continuum

In this section the ecofemiotic understanding of spatio-temporal relativity that contributes to interconnectedness is examined in the select folktales.

Stories represent a microcosm. They exist in a space-time continuum. They provide us an opportunity to interrogate the mechanistic understanding of space-time in contrast to the space-time consciousness of nonhuman life. In the indigenous and folk narratives, land, water, the elements, the sun, the moon, and the stars are beyond human space-time. However, they follow a natural rhythm and pattern of their own. Gaia Care Narratives provide a clarion call to these life-affirming motifs in folktales that can help humans to mimic these patterns to promote love and care for the well-being of the planet. "Avvaiyar's Rest" is a Tamil legend that is centered on eco-spirituality. As the *Cankam* poet Avvaiyar rests under a tree she sits with her legs pointed toward the temple. When the priest informs her about it, Avvaiyar told him, "I will be delighted to move them away from the god. Simply tell me in which direction there is no god, and there will I point my feet" (Macdonald 92). The story reiterates the *Akam* concept that connects the heart with the Earth, the microcosm with the macrocosm. It distinguishes human space-time with Nature's space-time which represents a continuum. Avvaiyar the *Cankam* poet represents the qualities of Mother Earth or Gaia. She is aware of the earth-centric, nature-centric, space-time continuum. Such tales help us to revisualize an alternative space-time in a world dominated by mechanistic outlook and hence form a Gaia Care Narrative.

Patterns in nature are often circular. The study attempts to revisit nature's patterns that help us humans to identify and integrate synchronous networks. "The Man Who Planted Trees" is an allegorical short story that deals with an old shepherd's attempt to reforest a valley in the foothills of Alps.

> After the midday meal he resumed his planting. I suppose I must have been fairly insistent in my questioning, for he answered me. For three years he had been planting trees in this wilderness. He had planted one hundred thousand. Of the hundred thousand, twenty thousand had expected to lose half, to rodents or to the unpredictable designs of Providence. There remained ten thousand oak trees to grow where nothing had grown before.
>
> (Giono 3)

Several folktales across the world abound with the motif of reforesting the place for the benefit of future generations. The act of tree-planting as an event happens in the space-time continuum. The story represents a regenerative *akam* envisioned and put into practice by an individual for the sake of the Earth community.

The term "topophilia" was coined by the geographer Yi-Fu Tuan of the University of Wisconsin and is defined as the affective bond with one's environment – a person's mental, emotional, and cognitive ties to a place. According to Tuan, "topophilia and environment . . . mutually contribute to the formation of values" (3). Tuan establishes the connection between spatial location and social identity thus: In ordinary usage, place means primarily two things: one's position in society and spatial location. The study of status belongs to sociology whereas the study of location belongs to geography. Yet clearly the two meanings overlap to a large degree: one seems to be a metaphor for the other (408). The love for the landscape in the folktales as Gaia Care Narratives reinvigorates the mindscape which in turn inspires the humans to transform and envision a better Earthscape for the future generations.

In the Tamil folktale "Tell It to the Walls" translated by AK Ramanujan an old widow is unhappy with her sons and daughters-in-law at her *akam*. One day she left the house seeking peace in the *puram*. She found an old dilapidated house. She started telling her woes to the walls in front of her, and the walls broke down one by one. When she poured out all her feelings, she felt lighter in body and spirit. Then she returned to her *akam*, finding peace in both her heart and household. The story moves from an oppressive *akam* to a transformative *akam* at the end of the tale. Folktales signify circular patterns in both content and structure. As folklorists like Propp have explored, folktales often begin with the journey of the protagonist from his/her *akam* and end with the return to their *akam*.

One of the aims of the ecological approach is to relink the dots and reweave patterns that work toward the wellbeing of all life forms. The "Ant and the Grasshopper" fable posits the message of hard work and planning for the future. The story can be interpreted in different ways. In concurrence with the space-time continuum of nature the fable can be read as a clarion call to safeguard the resources in the finite planet. At the same time the story also promotes a materialistic outlook where there is more emphasis on accumulating the resources that are meant for all living beings in the environment. The fable can be interpreted as a tale of mindfulness or living in the present moment.

In India, right from the childhood days women especially in the rural areas were introduced to practice the art of drawing *kolams* (a line drawing or floral diagram) drawn by connecting the dots at the entrance of homes. *Kolams* are symbols of abundance. Traditionally, the rural women create *kolams* using rice flour to provide food for ants and tiny insects. Systems Thinking resembles a beautiful *Kolam* drawn at the threshold of the house, as a symbol of a new dawn and an awakening. Academicians and researchers are often preoccupied with analysis, breaking down the whole into parts. Alternatively, systems thinking differs from other courses as it tries to synthesize the theories, philosophies, and belief systems that converge together to form a meaningful whole. The synthesis of biological, cognitive, social, and ecological dimensions creates a strong foundation for the learners to identify the systemic problems and offer systemic solutions. Gaia Care Narrative aims at a unique system thinking model that is fortified by the worldview of abundance and benevolence akin to the earth-centered philosophies of people who live close to nature.

Systems thinking inspires us to look at patterns and networks at different levels. The link between humans as the microcosm connected to the planet as the macrocosm is understood using the concept of social understanding of autopoiesis. Autopoiesis is a term derived from biology that means "self-creation" or "self-organization". According to Lovelock, Gaia is a "self-regulating" living being. The identification of the web of life in "Systems Thinking" has very close resemblance to indigenous ecofeminism and folklore. They share common threads like interconnectedness, interdependence, and cyclical pattern of life. Autopoiesis throws light upon a deep understanding of the body and mind (as a whole) that signifies the microcosm of the macrocosm. In classical Tamil poetics the concept of *Akam* (meaning interior) and *Puram* (meaning exterior). The systems change within *Akam* (self as the part of the whole) will positively affect change in *Puram* (society and development).

"The Mosquito Extermination Project" is a folktale from India which Margaret Read MacDonald categorizes under the topic "All Things Are Connected". It is a parable on reductionism. The story interrogates the cosmetic changes and the superficial measures taken by the humans in power that do not offer long-term holistic systemic solutions to the environment and society. When a city is "beset by mosquitoes" (79), they introduce "buckets of frogs" (79) to exterminate them. Mosquitoes disappear, but there were frogs everywhere. Then the humans introduce the snakes. The frogs vanish, but there "were snakes everywhere" (80). Finally, "the people had to abandon that city and move elsewhere" (80). This ecological story can be examined using a systems view of life. The narrator has love for humankind and cares for the wellbeing of the planet. This Gaia Care Narrative underscores the deep-rooted problems in our society and the divisive *akam* and our environment and provides a holistic outlook of life for a transformative and a regenerative *akam*.

Gaia Care Narratives aim at reweaving the space-time relationship. Returning to the basics and revaluing the motifs and patterns on the intrinsic worth is a way of re-joining sacredness of life. In terms of space-time, it reawakens the consciousness of the parts of the whole and renews the different components of the Earth family. By remodeling and integrating the alternative worldviews Gaia Care Narratives helps us to restructure deep networks. The identification of the different types of *akam* the mind with *akam* the world, the folktales attempt to create avenues toward an alternative socio-economic order characterized by love, parity, and justice.

Critically examining the Spatio-Temporal Relativity in folktales promotes interconnectedness and fosters Gaia Care Principles in the following ways: They help us to revisualize an indigenous nature-centered space-time by interrogating human view of space and time. By revisiting nature's patterns in the folktales, it is possible to identify and integrate synchronous networks that contribute to social and ecological balance. This is done by relinking motifs and patterns that work toward the wellbeing of all life forms on earth. The wisdom narratives of the indigenous people pave way toward the reconciliation with our planet as integrated and significant parts of the whole. As a first step it is necessary to review the storyscape as a way of understanding indigenous wisdom. Consequently, it creates avenues toward reviving the earthscape through storytelling as environmental discourse. Folktales initiate the process of redialing circular principles by interrogating binaries and linear patterns. By comparing the mainstream worldviews with the alternative worldviews, it is possible to reverse the systemic problems that oppress environment and the socially marginalized. Folktales challenge fragmentation and reductionism and reassure interconnectedness of life by reconstructing earth designs that work in favor of sustainability and balance. The following section throws light upon the second dimension of Gaia Care Narratives namely Naturo-Cultural Density.

Nature-Culture Proximity

This section gives an account of nature-cultural density that contributes to the spirit of interdependence in the folktales chosen for study.

Folktales help us to redeem the deep-rooted networks and patterns that affirm life. By redeeming the nature's patterns, it is possible to understand and reaffirm a human culture centered on nature. "How the Kangaroo Got Its Pouch" is an Australian aboriginal tale that highlights the kindness of a Mother Kangaroo toward a wobbly wombat in trouble. In the process of saving the wobbly wombat the little Joey finds himself in trouble. Biamee the Creator spirit recognizes the compassion of the Mother Kangaroo and blesses her with a pouch to carry the young Joey. The story ends with these words, When the Kangaroo Mother thought about her pouch she said, "This really isn't fair! I am the only kangaroo with a pouch. What about my cousins and relatives? What about the wallabys, and the rat kangaroos? What about them?" (McKay 63) Biamee agreed with the Kangaroo Mother and, because she thought of others, Biamee allowed pouches to grow on all the gentle marsupial mothers throughout the whole world. So, because of that gentle Kangaroo Mother's kindness, all the kangaroos gained pouches, way back when the world was young. Through the kind act of the mother kangaroo toward the wobbly wombat and the blessings she receives in turn from the creator spirit Biamee the story reiterates the spirit of interconnectedness and the circular pattern of life. In this story the hunter is an intruder who disturbs the harmony of the forest. The mother kangaroo works to bring about a balance. The mother kangaroo signifies the worldview of abundance.

The mother kangaroo shows love for her child and also the other living beings around her. In the same way, Biamee the creator also has love for all the living beings on Earth and represents a celebrative *akam*. Sherry Ortner in her essay, "Is Female to Male as Nature Is to Culture" explains,

> Now the categories of "nature" and "culture" are of course conceptual categories – one can find no boundary out in the actual world between the two states or realms of being. And there is no question that some cultures articulate a much stronger opposition between the two categories than others – it has even been argued that primitive peoples (some or all) do not see or intuit any distinction between the human cultural state and the state of nature at all.
>
> (6)

Interestingly, when one attempts to study the relation between nature and culture in *Cankam* poetry through the Ecofeminist lens, she/he comes across two levels of understanding. On one level, in the words of Sherry Ortner, the society poses "the problem of the universal devaluation of women" (69). On the other hand, the concept of *Tinai* at a larger level aligns with the beliefs of the Ecofeminist ideals represented through the signs and symbols quite specifically through the explicit comparisons (similes) and implicit comparisons (metaphors).

Abundance is the worldview of humans who live close to nature. The following anecdote upholds the spirit of abundance. The teacher had accompanied her ecocriticism students to a hill station. One of the students had bought a coat in one of the shops in a tourist spot. He had paid the money but forgot to collect the coat. They visited several places during the day. When they were returning to their hotel in the evening, somebody stopped their van. It was the shopkeeper. He entered the van and spotted the student who had bought the coat. He returned the coat with a smile. The students and the teacher were overwhelmed by the act of the simple person who lived in close proximity with nature and represented the earth-centered values of love, care, and contentment. The anecdote represents a celebrative *akam* and through the act of storytelling inspires a transformative, regenerative *akam* in the minds of the listeners.

"Mikku and the Trees" is a folktale from Estonia that reaffirms nature-culture interdependence. When Mikku goes into the forest to gather firewood, the trees request him not to cut them down. Mikku respects the words of the trees and shows love and concern toward them. And the trees bless him and sing,

"You care for us . . . and we will care for you
You care for us . . . and we will care for you".
(Macdonald 24)

The trees signify Earth's continuum with their seasonal cycles. Mikku humanizes the event and integrates himself with Mother Nature's harmonious existence. He represents a culture where nature is at the center. He respects the sacredness and the intrinsic value of trees and epitomizes the worldview of abundance. Together they contribute to a new socio-economic order characterized by interdependence and peaceful coexistence. In the Tamil folktale "The Hunter and the Elephant", the elephant represents Gaia's love for her children, an example of interactive or collaborative *akam*. However, the materialistic hunter attempts to kill the elephant for acquiring the tusks. When the elephant realizes the truth, he tries to teach a lesson to man.

"Three Green Ladies" is a folktale from England that signifies human love for the trees in their environment. The father and the younger brother respect the intrinsic value of trees. The two elder brothers however represent the dominant materialistic consumerist society. They cut down two of those trees as they "chopped at the heart of the tree" (Macdonald 3) the youngest brother, "worked the land well and it prospered. And every evening he would climb the hill and sit for a while in the shade of the One Green Lady" (Macdonald 6). These tales help us to resist materialism and dominant systems that oppress environment and the marginalized groups. In turn it provides an impetus to reassess nature-centrism. Folktales based on natural phenomenon confirm nature's patterns of abundance and promote nature-culture fortified by benevolence.

Through folktales as Gaia Care Narratives, it is possible to review the story-scape and understand indigenous wisdom. In the Tamil folktale on "The Clouds and Stars" the quintessential aspect of respecting one's time and space is represented through the transformation of clouds into rain and stars into fireflies. From a deep ecological perspective, the folktale can be re-read as a parable of reverence to the intrinsic value or sacredness of life. At the end of the story the clouds and the stars feel their place is in the sky. Both experience the oppressive *akam* in the hands of humans and find regeneration at the end of the tale.

All living beings have a purpose to live on this planet. Gaia Care Narratives reaffirm nature-culture by examining the mutual support and co-operation of human and nonhuman beings on this earth. "Who Is Greater" is a Tamil folktale that projects an anthropocentric viewpoint of hierarchy on flora and fauna. In the tale there is an argument between two birds, the parrot and the crow and the two trees, mango and neem. Humans tend to be biased toward other living organisms based on the utilitarian value and definitions of beauty. The parrot and the peacock are considered beautiful creatures compared to the black crow and the cuckoo. The sweetness of the mangoes is seen superior to the bitterness of the neem, though the humans know that the neem has more medicinal value than mango. The story represents hierarchies in man-made culture and a divisive *akam*. When we revisit the culture of nature, we understand that elements in nature are unbiased. The rain, the breeze, and the sunshine do not show bias to any living or nonliving beings on the planet. The story signifies the need for a transformative and regenerative *akam*. Hence Gaia Care Narratives attempt to underscore heterarchical relations in nature-culture. Nature and culture conglomerate into a meaningful whole in the process of storytelling.

The systemic conception of nature is reinforced by understanding the connection between science and spirituality. The connection between science and spirituality is reiterated by Capra's time-tested study of bridging modern physics and eastern mysticism. The distinction between religion and spirituality and the connection between spirituality and mysticism enlightens us to see the world and revere the intrinsic value and sacredness of life around us. Lumerai, the Mother Snake called the Rainbow Serpent Creation Story is an Australian aboriginal tale from the Northern territory. In this creation story the rainbow serpent is the creator who awakens life on Earth. She nurtures the rainforests with "milk from her breasts soaked into Earth" (41). In this way the creator awakens the animals, birds, and the first humans. The narrator notes,

> And the mother snake taught them their tribal ways: to share with one another and take only what they needed to live and respect Earth itself. She taught them to respect the spirit of all things; the trees, the rocks, and the creatures because all have a spiritual dreaming.

(42)

The mother creator represents the spirit of interconnectedness and contributes to the spatio-temporal relativity of the tale. The organic relationship between the creator and the created reflects the theme of interdependence, signifies nature-cultural density, and exemplifies a regenerative *akam*. The symbol of motherhood and mothering lends itself to the respect for the intrinsic value of life forms and signifies the spirituo-physical gravity.

"Finding the Center" is an Ojibway tale which can be re-read as Gaia Care Narrative that highlights the core, the nucleus, or the embryo of life's existence where the Great Spirit gifts the humans with a bundle,

Cherish wisdom	Live peacefully
Respect all life	Honor your promises
Be courageous	Be honest
Live moderately	Share your gifts
	(Macdonald 91)

These authentic words of wisdom shape the worldview of the eco-storytellers and the listeners to envision an alternative socio-economic order based on justice and integrity. In this way it is possible to restructure deep networks and revere earth-based spirituality. By retuning the discordant notes Gaia Love Narratives reverberate intrinsic creativity to recreate a world characterized by social and environmental justice in unison with a transformative, regenerative *akam*.

Gaia Care Narratives attempt to bridge nature and culture where stories also become "interbeings". It attempts to find earth-centered motifs and patterns that are already a part of the cultural process of the human beings who are narrating the tale, listening to the tale, reading a tale, or writing a tale and as a result as Thich Nhat Hanh puts it, "the insight of interbeing has the power to wake us up" (2). When humans understand the "inter-be" connection with the subjects of nature, they contribute the mindful ways to Gaia Care Narratives. "When we try to pick out anything by itself", said John Muir, "we find it hitched to everything else in the universe" (Ingram et al. 11). This spirit of interconnectedness inspires us to revisit and revive indigenous stories as Gaia Care Narratives.

Naturo-cultural density encourages interdependence in folktales as Gaia Care Narratives. The following principles enable such a process. The study of folktales enables the redemption of nature's motifs in life-affirming cultural narratives. The indigenous narratives reaffirm nature-culture by examining mutuality among life forms. Earth-centered folktales can be re-read to understand inherent culture among the nonhuman beings in nature. As a result, it enables humans to redefine the nature of a new regenerative earth-centric culture. Folktales initiate a consciousness-raising process to understand the needs of the environment and regulate the use of flora and fauna as material resources. By identifying the interconnections and interrelationships folktale as a microcosm helps us to regenerate an earth-centric lifeworld. By identifying the role of fauna and flora in folktales Gaia Care Narratives help us to reimagine benevolence as a way out of ecological chaos and misery. Practically speaking the folktales offer innovative ideas to reexamine sustenance from the point of view of the marginalized. By reconsidering interdependence as a path toward sustainable living, folktales resonate earth's philosophy in different aspects of human culture that can be transformed into reflective action. The following section deals with the study of spirituo-physical gravity in folktales as an environmental discourse.

Spirit-Matter Connection

In this section the spirituo-physical gravity that acknowledges the intrinsic value is explored in the select folktales.

"Hidden Divinity" is a folktale from India which emphasizes the importance of revaluing the intrinsic worth or sacredness of life. It confirms the belief in *Akam*-Zen faith in the soul as the microcosm of the macrocosm. When Brahma decided to "hide the human's divinity in a place where the humans would never find it" (Macdonald 93). "Some suggested the depths of the sea. But they knew humans would dive even to the bottom of the sea and find it. Some suggested the tops of the mountains" (Macdonald 93). But finally, Brahma exclaimed, "We will place human divinity deep inside of each human. They will never think of looking there" (Macdonald 93). As Margaret Read Macdonald explains that, "this story suggests that our better nature may lie deep within ourselves" (93) which needs to be explored in this era of environmental crisis. The tale as Gaia Care Narrative reiterates the importance of turning inward and looking at the significance of a regenerative *akam* as the organizing principle of life on this planet.

One of the predominant concerns of this ecological approach is to identify ways to regulate the use of resources by understanding the needs of the environment. For example, in the Japanese folktale, "Why the Sea Water Is Salty" there are two brothers, one is kind and the other guilty. The kind brother signifies the worldview of abundance and the mean brother signifies the worldview of scarcity. Folktales based on natural phenomenon emphasize the importance of nonhuman life forms on this planet as not mere resources for human use. In this way it is possible to regenerate earth-centric lifeworld by understanding interrelationships.

Gaia Care Narratives promote environmental cognition and understanding. Life and cognition are seen inseparable. Continuous learning and adaptation results in continual structural changes. The relationship among perception, emotion, and behavior is also established. In the context of cognition and soul Capra integrates the concepts of *Atman*, *Anima* and the Psyche and Breath, *Spiritus*, *Pneuma*, and *Ruah* (The Systems View of Life 277). *Akam* can also signify the *Atman* and the *Anima* that shape the consciousness of humans to act with ecological intelligence. Mind is no longer seen as an entity but a process. The two types of consciousness namely primary or core consciousness and higher-order or reflective consciousness lend itself to emergence and create new avenues toward the understanding of systemic cognitive experience in Gaia Care Narratives.

How do we reshape eco-cognition to challenge and counter a materialistic outlook? A story the author heard as a child goes like this. A man went to God and asked, "What's the value of life?" God gave him a stone and told him to find out the value of the stone but not to sell it. The man took it to the orange seller and the orange seller said that it was worth 12 oranges. The man apologized to the orange seller and said he cannot sell it. Then he met a vegetable seller who said it was worth a sack of potatoes. The man said he cannot sell it and apologized to him. Then he took it to the jewelry shop. The shopkeeper said the stone was worth 50 lakhs. The man said he was not supposed to sell it and left the place. Then the man went to a shopkeeper who sold precious stones. The shopkeeper said that it was a ruby stone and it was priceless. The man thanked him and left the place. Humans value things and people only based on their level of information and understanding. The folktale outlines the intrinsic value of all matter on this planet and confirms the importance of a transformative *akam*. The story also highlights the importance of reshaping the eco-cognition of people by challenging a materialistic consumerist outlook.

Folktales as Gaia Care Narratives help the storytellers, listeners, and readers to reimagine benevolence as a way out of the ecological chaos and misery. The feminists have often contended with the portrayal of protagonists and antagonists in fairytales as stereotypes of angel in the house and monster. Gaia Care Narratives acknowledge the problems of stereotyping, yet it attempts to highlight elements of goodness in all those characters that promote peaceful coexistence. Cinderella is sensitive to the needs of her environment. Though she experiences the divisive *akam* she believes in creating a collaborative *akam* to bring about transformation and regeneration. She provides food for rats. She waters the plants in her garden. She saves the deer from the huntsman. Her sensitivity and kindness toward her fellow beings is acknowledged by humans and nonhuman beings around her. Fairytales can be re-read as Gaia Care Narratives by highlighting the different types of *akam* in them.

"Love the Weeds" is a folktale that helps us to reexamine sustenance from the point of view of the marginalized, the silenced, the oppressed, and the other. The word "weed" is an anthropocentric term that classifies certain plants based on the utilitarian value that emerges from a divisive *akam*. Gaia Care Narratives attempt to acknowledge the sacredness of every tiny living creature, plant, insect, and rocks to create a transformative *akam* that acknowledges all life forms. Based on a consumerist culture and materialistic outlook humans tend to categorize certain plants as weeds.

"The Blind Man and the Elephant" is a parable of multiple perspectives. In this study the tale is re-read as a parable of pluralism, diversity, and interdependence as a path toward sustainable living. Each and every individual perspective of the six blind men are important to find the complete picture of the animal. Each one had a perspective of his own which was often decoded as a divisive *akam*. But together they contributed to the larger picture in terms of a collaborative *akam* that results in a regenerative *akam*. In this way, Gaia Care Narratives resonate earth's philosophy in different aspects of human culture. Humans can acknowledge nature-culture by reawakening eco-consciousness among children and youth for a better future. By humanizing the environment, they can contribute to the peace and harmony of the nature-centered living. Humans can renew earth family with respect, compassion, and stewardship.

Folktales help us to reconcile with earth spirituality to recreate a culture of love and care. In the Tamil folktale "The Princess and the Parrots" the queen and her family respect the intrinsic value of the girl child. They protect her from the manacles of patriarchy and the parrots come to her rescue. They act as foster parents and provide a collaborative *akam*. When the king realizes his mistake, the narrative signifies a transformative *akam* and the girl returns to the palace, her home, her *akam* which indicates the circular pattern of life.

Humans who live close to nature believe in sacredness of life forms. This idea is substantiated in the following anecdote. It was a hilly town where people lived together as kith and kin. There was a mosque in the first street, a church in the second street, and a temple in the third street. The people believed in different religions, but they all lived as one community as they not only drew sustenance from the forests but also the culture of diversity and pluralism from nature. One day a mischievous tourist made a garland of slippers and laid it in front of a deity in the temple. When the local people came to know they got together, understood the intention of the miscreants and threw the slippers away and went back to work. The story drives home their respect for life and their belief in eco-spirituality as earth-based spirituality.

Humans signify the microcosm of the macrocosm. The intricate connection between the humans and the planet is reinforced by the following anecdote. An auto-rickshaw driver asked a teacher why the earth experienced so much of scorching heat, catastrophe like tsunami, and destructions like earthquakes. The teacher answered: Scientists have answers to explain "How all those things happen on earth". However, to answer the question why, one should see the relationship among the five senses of human beings and the five elements of the universe. When human persons are good at using their senses (eyes, ears, mouth, nose, and touch), they spread goodness all around them as waves. It, in turn, maintains harmony, peace, and tranquility in nature and its five elements (air, space, soil, water, fire, and wind). When human beings do evil deeds, nature imitates them and natural calamities destroy much and many. In this anecdote, the scientist aims to affirm the significance of a collaborative and transformative *akam*.

Spirituo-physical gravity inspires respect for intrinsic value in the folktales with the following principles: Folktales allow us to reinvent the mindscape to explore eco-sensitivity and eco-spirituality through life-affirming motifs and patterns. The indigenous narratives resist dominant systems that treat earth and the marginalized as matter. By identifying the spiritual element in matter, the folktales enable a reshaping of eco-cognition to challenge and counter materialistic outlook. As a result, it paves way toward re-joining sacredness as a way out of the global challenges that oppress life. By examining the destructive notes that harm nature and marginalized groups folktales retune discordant notes into harmonious tunes in accord with nature.

The next chapter throws light upon the significance of folktales as Gaia Care Narratives in a classroom by establishing storytelling as a form of environmental pedagogy.

4   Storytelling as Eco-Pedagogy

Classroom as *Akaram*

The chapter deals with the theory and practice of storytelling as an environmental pedagogy. The word *Aka(Pu)ram* or *Akaram* is an amalgamation of *Akam* and *Puram*, and *Akaram* the portmanteau term also refers to the first letter of the Tamil alphabet அ that signifies a new beginning. The classroom as a site of eco-pedagogy bridges the gap between *Akam* the interior world and *Puram* the exterior world. According to John Paul Tassoni, "Ecofeminism offers a better approach to life than the anthropomorphic, androcentric conceptions of nature that dominate western culture" (Gaard and Murphy 204). Through the storytelling process as eco-pedagogy, the participants can become, "active forces in the construction and maintenance of the heterarchical, holistic societies that ecofeminists promote" (Gaard and Murphy 204). The participants in the eco-storytelling process can "engage critically with and consider alternatives to those aspects of our society that undermine egalitarian relations not only between humans – but also between humans and nonhumans and among the various other forms of life on the planet" (Gaard and Murphy 205). Hence, the folktale as Gaia Care Narrative is used to promote the spirit of the abundance, interconnectedness, interdependence, intrinsic value, and cyclical pattern of life.

Primarily, Gaia Care Narratives as consciousness-raising tools promote storytelling as a mindful method of environmental pedagogy. It emphasizes the importance of "now" or the present moment in relation to the past and the future. They underscore the cyclical pattern of life. But unfortunately, the youth of today are unaware of the bigger picture. They are grappling with the bits and pieces of the giant jigsaw puzzle in a hasty manner. Through storytelling one can rekindle the passion to narrate holistic stories of heirloom that are productive to the person and his/her society. These narratives promote the process of praxis where reflective stories end up as responsible action. On the other hand, the stories that do not inspire people into action can be called dead stories. They do not have life in them. The affirmative Gaia Care Narratives as living seeds are fortified and nurtured by the power of love and care for fellow beings in this planet.

DOI: 10.4324/9781003406686-5

Most importantly, Paulo Freire's concept of dialogic pedagogy is at the fulcrum of the study. Freire elucidates,

> As we attempt to analyse dialogue as a human phenomenon, we discover something which is the essence of dialogue itself: the word . . . Within the word we find two dimensions, reflection and action, in such radical interaction that if one is sacrificed-even in part-the other immediately suffers. There is no true word that is not at the same time a praxis. Thus, to speak a true word is to transform the world.
>
> (87)

Eco-storytelling is identified as a form of dialogic pedagogy to inspire humans to be sensitive to the needs of our environment. Dialogic pedagogy promotes critical thinking, radical insights, and multiple interpretations of folktales as ecological narratives. While banking method "effaces student's own cultural experiences" (Gaard and Murphy 207), the proposed method of eco-pedagogy acknowledges, networks, and promotes the cultural factors of all the participants in the classroom.

The Anishinaabe tale narrated by Kathleen Westcott provides an alternative discourse on woman-tree proximity. When a young woman loses her husband, she goes into the forest and finds refuge under a birch bark tree. She stayed there for two years in total stillness. Human history tells us that Gautama Buddha found enlightenment under the Bodhi tree in the lap of mother nature. Similarly, the woman buddha in the Anishinaabe tale finds a moment of enlightenment under the birch bark tree after two years of solitude, meditation, and contemplation. She heard a voice from the birch bark tree. The narrator describes,

> And the tree is saying, "My Grand-daughter, I've held you all these months. I've come to know you well. I've come to know your devotion to your people and the strong bond that you carry with your husband. I know that you've lost your will to live and that your desire to drop your body and cross over to join your husband is strong. At the same time, your desire to be of some use to your people is also strong, and it has always been there".
>
> (Doerfler et al. 65)

The grandmother tree teaches the woman to get the bark of the tree without doing harm, in an *Ahimsa* way to make birch bark baskets. Similarly, she teaches her to acquire "basswood for sewing and willow for framing" (Doerfler et al. 65). This life-affirming tale represents Gaia Care Narrative as it is characterized by a high level of spatio-temporal relativity, greater value of nature-cultural density, and deeper quality of spirituo-physical gravity. And together the grandmother tree and the woman create an alternative socio-economic order based on gift economy and doughnut economy. There is a circular pattern that characterizes the entire story as the woman returns to her village to provide sustainable living for herself and for the people and environment around her.

Storytelling as Environmental Praxis

The following section gives an account of an eco-storytelling experiment conducted at the tertiary level of education. Kathleen Westcott's Anishinaabe tale was used in the experiment.

The principles of *Akam* poetics, the ecofemiotics framework, and the theory of folktales as Gaia Care Narratives were used as guiding principles in understanding the five stages of mindfulness, mediation, mapping, manifesto, and mission. Thirty students were introduced to the ecofemiotic framework and the three-dimensional concepts of space-time that contributes to interconnectedness, nature-culture that promotes interdependence, and spirit-matter that highlights intrinsic value which in turn is envisioned as a path toward emergence and a society-economy based on sustainability and ecological balance.

Gaia Care Narratives can be identified as an educational tool in the twenty-first century. In his article, "Vertical Literacy: Reimagining the 21st-Century University" Otto Scharmer enumerates 12 principles of "what a 21st century university" would look like. They are: (1) Transforming Society and Self with an awareness to shift from "ego to eco" consciousness; (2) Learning as kindling of a flame by creating environments for "deep listening practices"; (3) Action learning where the students learn by doing; (4) Whole person learning that activates an open mind, heart, and will; (5) The learners as ecosystem leaders; (6) Self-knowledge that includes listening, contemplation, mindfulness, and social-emotional learning practices; (7) Systems thinking to map individuals, groups, organizations, and societal systems; (8) Learners and change-makers to be literate in the social arts and aesthetic practices; (9) A scientific approach to view one's self in relation to the world; (10) Create awareness-based social technologies; (11) Democratize: build infrastructures for deep learning at scale; (12) Cultivating generative social fields – The Reggio Emilia approach is known for seeing place as the third teacher (with the learner and the educator being the first two). Building on that foundation, we have come to see the cultivation of generative social fields, of relationships among learners, educators, parents, community members, and nature, as a powerful gateway to the deeper sources of knowing ("the fourth teacher") (Scharmer). As consciousness-raising discourse Gaia Care Narratives emerge as an ecological-semiotic praxis that reshapes the mind and consciousness of the humans for a better planet. It aims to promote Eco-literacy and Systemic Thinking. The students are introduced to the different dimensions of the proposed ecofemiotic framework and the scope of folktales as Gaia Care Narratives.

The folktales identified as Gaia Care Narratives using the proposed network are put into use at five stages namely mindfulness, mediation, mapping, manifesto, and mission which form a cyclical process of ecological consciousness-raising. Love is at the center of the proposed dialogic pedagogical framework. As Paulo Freire explains,

> Founding itself upon love, humility and faith, dialogue becomes a horizontal relationship of which mutual trust between the dialogues is the logical consequence. It would be a contradiction in terms of dialogue – loving, humble, and full of faith – did not produce this climate of mutual trust between the dialoguers into ever closer partnership in the naming of the world.
>
> (91)

Interestingly, the process of eco-storytelling draws inspiration from the "horizontal relationship" (91) proposed by Freire and vertical literacy of Scharmer to form an eco-pedagogy that is envisioned at five levels: Stage 1 – Mindfulness includes exploration of themes, motifs, and patterns of abundance, interconnectedness, interdependence, intrinsic value, and cyclical pattern of life in the chosen folktale as Gaia Care Narrative; Stage 2 – Mediation requires recognition of systemic problems that affect our society, economy, and our environment; Stage 3 – Mapping: The systemic problems that affect our planet are mapped with the systemic solutions in the folktales as Gaia Care Narratives. Stage 4 – Manifesto where the humans as responsible citizens of the Earth come up with practical ways of tackling the man-made problems in our environment. Stage 5 – Mission where the storytelling process lends itself to consciousness-raising and emergence. The process of storytelling is envisioned as a cyclical process where the environmental mission will re-energize and re-invigorate another set of mindful thinkers and practitioners in the future. The storytelling exercise is visualized as an imaginative project for 100 years. The first two decades deal with mindfulness, the second two decades deal with mediation, the third two decades deal with mapping, the fourth two decades contribute to the manifesto, and the last two decades foresee the actual mission.

The participants in the storytelling process visualize themselves as earth warriors attempting to mend the ways of humans to be sensitive to the needs of the environment around them. Stage 1 Mindfulness: In the first stage of mindful eco-storytelling and questioning the participants listened to the stories, generate mindful questions, and found answers in the following manner. The signs and symbols, motifs, and patterns (creation, time, seasons, space, directions, land, water, flora, fauna, totem, elements, lifeworld, relationships, connection, manifestation, etc.) in the story act as tools of ecological consciousness-raising. Stage 2 Mediation: At this stage of eco-storytelling process the participants visualize the two decades where the environmental

Table 4.1 Gaia Care Narratives in praxis visualized by the author in this study

Gaia Care Narratives in praxis	Phase I Mindfulness	Phase II Mediation	Phase III Mapping	Phase IV Manifesto	Phase V Mission
Spatio-Temporal Relativity	Creation, Time, Seasons, Space, Directions, Continuum	Reductionism	Holism	Moderation	Narrative of Interconnectedness
Naturo-Cultural Density	Land, Water, Flora, Fauna, Totem, Elements, Lifeworld	Greed	Contentment	Simplicity	Narrative of Interdependence
Spirituo-Physical Gravity	Relationships, Connection, Manifestation	Fragmentation	Interbeing	Respect	Narrative of Intrinsic value
Socio-Economic Parity	Sustainability, Emergence, Networks, Peaceful Coexistence	Scarcity	Abundance	Gratitude	Narrative of Emergence

issues and the socio-economic problems, such as reductionism, greed, frag-mentation, and scarcity, are identified and interrogated as eco-conscious responsible citizens of the planet. The participants highlighted systemic prob-lems that linked gender concerns, environmental issues, economic problems, and social injustice. Based on the Anishinaabe tale the participants identi-fied the social structures that are dominated by patriarchy, materialism, and consumerist outlook. The binary opposition of man and woman, nature and culture, and spirit and matter are interrogated in the process using the eco-spiritual *Akam* philosophy and the ecofemiotic framework. The eco-storyteller dons the role of mediator who creates the space to identify the systemic prob-lems that exist in our society and environment. Stage 3 Mapping: The third stage dealt with the mapping of systemic problems with systemic solutions that include holism, contentment, interbeing, and abundance. The dominant mainstream worldviews were countered by the indigenous worldviews and effectively moderated by the educator's worldviews. Through the ecofemi-otic framework the Anishinaabe tale is read as a Gaia Care Narrative. The participants mapped folktales and indigenous narratives based on environ-mental movements such as the Chipko movement and Green Belt Movement with the Anishinaabe tale. Stage 4 Manifesto: The fourth stage deals with the identification of themes such as moderation, simplicity, respect, and gratitude that contribute to the manifesto for constructive ecological action. The par-ticipants highlighted the importance of nurture and protection of trees and forests, alternative forms of gift, and doughnut economy taking a cue from the sustainable eco-friendly products represented in the tale. Stage 5 Mis-sion: The fifth phase focuses on the role and responsibility of humans to act as responsible citizens of the planet where the folktale represents a narrative of interconnectedness, interdependence, intrinsic value, and emergence. The responses of the participants in the storytelling process are documented here:

I   What does the tree signify in the story?

- Respondent 1: The tree signifies independence and self-sufficiency in the story. It gives the young woman and her community hope to tide through the sufferings of the world.
- Respondent 2: The tree is a symbol of love. It helps the women to recover from the death of her husband.
- Respondent 3: The tree in the story signifies the importance of nature in the lives of human beings. Nature is capable of healing and recharging humans with a sense of purpose and meaning.
- Respondent 4: Tree represents the personal development, uniqueness, and individual beauty. Just as the branches of a tree strengthen and grow upwards to the sky, we too grow stronger, striving for greater knowledge, wisdom, and new experiences as we move through life.

- Respondent 5: The tree signifies the spiritual cord that connects the woman with her society and the tree nation. It also emphasizes on the importance of the interdependence of nature and humans for a better life.
- Respondent 6: The tree symbolizes the compassion and the healing effect that Nature has toward us. I feel the tree also symbolizes our ancestors as we see the tree addressing the woman as "granddaughter".
- Respondent 7: The trees signify a symbol of retreat and recollection of one's own self.
- Respondent 8: The tree signifies the spiritual cord that connects the woman with her society and the tree nation and it also signifies independence and self-sufficiency.
- Respondent 9: The tree in the story signifies the importance of nature in the lives of human beings.
- Respondent 10: The tree signifies the spiritual connection between society and nature.

II What does the tree-woman relationship symbolize in the folktale?

- Respondent 1: It symbolizes hope, where the tree assists her in understanding the value of life and helps her to live out of her own dignity and willingness to stay alive.
- Respondent 2: Tree-woman relationship shows the dependence humans have on nature. Although humans take nature for granted, they are dependent on nature for food, clothing, and shelter. This dependence is necessary to sustain the life of humans. Usually, woman is symbolized as nature. It acts as a mother nature.
- Respondent 3: This tree is also part of nature which nurtures the woman as mother and lifts her up in her life. The tree-woman relationship in the folk tale signifies mother and daughter relationship.
- Respondent 4: The tree-woman relationship symbolizes the need for the community to embrace their roots. The elders understand the importance of tapping into the ancient reserve of knowledge and hence support her through her journey of discovery.
- Respondent 5: The tree-woman relationship symbolized in the folktale is a maternal one as the tree held the woman for two years akin to a grandmother. The tree even views the woman as her granddaughter.
- Respondent 6: The relationship between the tree and the woman symbolizes the interconnectedness and interdependence of humans and nature. And it also symbolizes the mother-child relationship between nature and us.
- Respondent 7: The tree-woman relationship symbolizes the close union between man and nature and how each of which is closely intertwined.
- Respondent 8: The tree-woman relationship symbolized in the folktale is a maternal one as the tree held the woman for two years akin to a grandmother, the tree even views the woman as her granddaughter. The elders understand the importance of conserving the nature.

- Respondent 9: Tree-woman proximity shows the dependence humans have on nature. Although humans take nature for granted, they are dependent on nature for food, clothing, and shelter. This dependence is necessary to sustain the life of humans.
- Respondent 10: Tree-woman connection symbolizes, it is a maternal one the tree held the woman for two years to a grandmother. It also views the woman in her granddaughter.

III What do the birch bark tree baskets signify in the tale?

- Respondent 1: It signifies strength and beauty; birch bark baskets signify hope in this tale. The woman in the story found out a sense of purpose and was able to continue her life as a normal person.
- Respondent 2: The baskets were referred to as beautiful which also signifies her own life which she found back with the help of nature.
- Respondent 3: The birch bark baskets signify hope of the woman in the story. When a woman loses hope, the tree helps the woman by giving hope in her life by teaching her how to make birch bark baskets.
- Respondent 4: The birch bark baskets signify the hope of the young woman that she has got to live the rest of her life.
- Respondent 5: The birch bark basket is a manifestation of ancient knowledge. It changes the community and its dynamics by its sheer introduction.
- Respondent 6: The birch bark baskets signify the restoration of the widow's will to live along with the skill to live a purposeful life.
- Respondent 7: The birch bark baskets symbolize hope. Birch trees usually symbolize rebirth, new beginnings, and growth, and the birch basket in this story also provides a rebirth and helps the woman grow in life.
- Respondent 8: The baskets signify a sense of gratitude and support which the woman has always shown toward her community.
- Respondent 9: The birch baskets signify the restoration of the widow's will to live along with the skill to live a purposeful life.
- Respondent 10: Birch bark baskets signify hope in this tale. The woman in the story found out a sense of purpose and was able to continue her life as a normal person.

IV What is the difference between a woman's position in the village/society and the forest/nature?

- Respondent 1: In the society women are treated as weaker gender, but in nature they are given more importance and respect.
- Respondent 2: Woman's position in the village/society was to get support from other people to run her life, but in the forest/nature, she has got hope and a strong will power to live her life.
- Respondent 3: In reference to this story, the position of women was portrayed differently in the village and forest. In the village, she was

dependent on her husband for a living and experienced a subordinate position like the typical society. But in the forest where rules of society don't exist, everyone is considered an equal. Hence, she learned to be independent and was able to lead a new life.

- Respondent 4: A woman in a typically patriarchal society/village always complements the roles of men. She isn't given the space to voice her independent opinions.
- Respondent 5: A woman in a forest, on the other hand, is her own person. There she doesn't need to adhere to the rules of society, but to the great, leveling instincts of nature.
- Respondent 6: In the society the woman's position is to be a good wife and a mother, but, in the forest, woman is given autonomy to do things on her own.
- Respondent 7: In the village she feels numb and hopeless as it was a place filled with grief, whereas in the forest, she feels at one with nature and regains her will to live. The forests comfort her and provide her solace.
- Respondent 8: In the contemporary society women are looked as second to men and only recently have things started to change for the better. Whereas in nature woman or femininity has always been considered as strong elements.
- Respondent 9: In the society, women are dependent on other people. In the forest, nature empowers them to live alone.
- Respondent 10: In the village, her position in a family is to be a good wife and a mother, but in forest a woman is given autonomy to lead an independent life in association with nature.

V What is the ecological relevance of the tale to contemporary times?

- Respondent 1: In contemporary times, we are living in modernized world and so we depend on technology to relieve our stress. The happiness given by technology is temporary and so we fall into depression again and again. But the happiness and consolation given by nature is permanent and meaningful which lasts forever. This was shown clearly in this story.
- Respondent 2: The tree teaches the woman to make birch bark baskets and gives her meaningful life. The ecological relevance of the tale of contemporary times is that nature will give us life and hope even by tearing itself apart.
- Respondent 3: The importance of nature is looked down in the contemporary times. Forests, trees, and animals are killed and humans are making the world a monopoly. This story gives a valuable lesson on the importance of nature which will help the contemporary society to reflect and introspect.

- Respondent 4: It is relevant to contemporary times as the young woman harvests the tree bark with consent and holistically. She does not go about destroying the resource, but rather uses what she needs sustainably.
- Respondent 5: The ecological relevance of the tale to contemporary times is the ability to manifest destiny through the help of nature.
- Respondent 6: The tale is a reminder that nature always has our back and that if we are kind to her, she will reciprocate the kindness. Being at one with nature is sometimes all the therapy that humans require. The relevance here is how retreating into nature can most probably help humankind to overcome its sufferings.
- Respondent 7: The ecological relevance of the tale to contemporary times is the ability to manifest destiny through the help of nature. The importance of nature is looked down in contemporary world. Forests, trees, and animals are killed and humans are making the world a monopoly.
- Respondent 8: This story gives a valuable lesson on the importance of nature which will help the contemporary society to reflect and introspect.
- Respondent 9: The story represents a home in nature. Tree considered the women as a granddaughter which represented that the forest or nature is a home and all the members of the nature community are family for humans.
- Respondent 10: The ecological relevance is the ability to manifest the destiny with the help of nature.

VI How are the eight types of *Akam* represented in the story?

- Respondent 1: There is no distinction between ritual and ordinary, the spiritual and reality or nature and humanity. They represent the celebrative *akam*, the interactive *akam*, and the transformative *akam*.
- Respondent 2: The story represents a home that supports one another, considers feelings of one another and a life which is fully depended on nature and peace. They represent all the eight types of akam namely the celebrative *akam*, the divisive *akam*, the passive *akam*, the oppressive *akam*, the interactive *akam*, the transformative *akam*, and the regenerative *akam*.
- Respondent 3: The birch tree becomes a temporary refuge for the widow during her grief over her loss of her husband. All the eight types of *akam* are found in the story.
- Respondent 4: The story presents nature and humans in a kith-kin relationship that allows freedom with responsibility. Though all the eight types of *akam* are there, the interactive *akam* is the most significant one in the story.

- Respondent 5: The *akam* represented here is that of a close-knit community where fishing might be the predominant occupation of the folks. All the eight types of *akam*.
- Respondent 6: The birch tree offers refuge to the widow and a new life for her future. All the eight types of *akam*.
- Respondent 7: All the four stages of *akam* are found in the folktale. All the eight types of *akam*.
- Respondent 8: The tree represents Mother Earth and shows the principles of nature-nurture. All the eight types of *akam*.
- Respondent 9: The story represents a home in nature. Tree considered the woman as a granddaughter which represented that the forest or nature is a home and all the members of the nature community are family for humans. All the eight types of *akam*.
- Respondent 10: The birch baskets represented a new means of living for the single mother in the society who is otherwise stuck in sorrow because of her dead husband. All the eight types of *akam*.

VII   What are the signs of interconnectedness in the tale?

- Respondent 1: Nature connectedness is the extent to which individuals include nature as part of their identity. It includes an understanding of nature and everything it is made up of, even the parts that are not pleasing.
- Respondent 2: In this story, when woman has no one to help her mentally and emotionally, this tree helps her to overcome her problems. The entire community is able to rally around her and offer her support in her period of mourning. Therefore, the community assumes the role of a big family that supports and looks out for each other. This is a symbol of interconnectedness. The woman who lost her husband lives in grief for one year found a tree and starts to live under it.
- Respondent 3: After one year she hears the voice of the tree. So, the life of human and nature is interconnected in the story.
- Respondent 4: The signs of interconnectedness in the tale are the communion between the birch and the widow as they share their thoughts by uttering a word while also forming a maternal bond.
- Respondent 5: The woman being drawn to the tree and sitting with her back to the tree and the tree being able to understand her thoughts and feelings and comforting her when she needed it are signs of interconnectedness present in the story.
- Respondent 6: Signs such as the various seasons of the year and how it is connected with an individual's life. Just as how winter is represented as a period of staying in, loss of a loved one is also seen as a time of solitude and introspection. The community in the story is a good sign of interconnectedness.

- Respondent 7: People were helpful for the woman to look after her family after her husband died. This shows how well attached and connected are they to each other. Also, the instance when the woman was drawn to the tree also represents the interconnection she felt for nature.
- Respondent 8: The communion between the birch and the widow, they share their thoughts by uttering a word because they are bonding a maternal bond.
- Respondent 9: The sign of interconnectedness in the tale is the communion between the birch and the widow as they share their thoughts by uttering a word while also forming a maternal bond.
- Respondent 10: The community in the story is a good sign of interconnectedness.

VIII What are the signs of interdependence in the tale?

- Respondent 1: All living things depend on their environment to supply them with what they need, including food, water, and shelter. This is known as interdependence.
- Respondent 2: The signs in the story are: Tree teaches woman to make birch bark basket; tree also provided shelter to the woman by allowing her to sit under it for so many days. The entire community is interdependent not only among themselves but also with the nature around it. They rely on the abundance of nature to sustain them in the fishing season. They also rely on the forest and flora around them for mental and material support. Thus, they become interdependent and a part of a holistic whole.
- Respondent 3: The story portrays that woman are dependent on their husbands and children are dependent on their mothers and every human is dependent on nature.
- Respondent 4: The signs of interdependence in the tale are the Anishinaabe community taking care of the widow's children during her grief and the birch tree consoling the widow while giving a purpose to live.
- Respondent 5: The birch tree sharing its own self to help the woman by teaching her to cut off its skin and make baskets out of them and similarly teaching her to gather basswood for sewing and willow for framing and the woman doing all this without killing the tree while reciprocating her gratitude signify their interdependence.
- Respondent 6: Just like how the woman needed the tree's wisdom to start making baskets, the community also needed the woman back. The signs of interdependence in the tale are the Anishinaabe community taking care of the widow's children during her grief and the birch tree consoling the widow while giving a purpose to live.

- Respondent 7: The community in which the woman lived represents the interdependence among the people. While the community helped her to take care of her children after her husband's death, the woman passed on the skills she learned from the tree to make a living. This shows the interdependency among people.
- Respondent 8: The Anishinaabe community taking care of the widow's children in her grief and the birch tree consoling the widow giving a purpose to live.
- Respondent 9: The woman loves the birch bark tree and the tree cares for the woman. Their love and care are translated into love and care for humankind.
- Respondent 10: Humans live close to nature and nature reciprocates the love to human beings which signifies interdependence.

IX How does the story represent nature-culture through different signs and symbols?

- Respondent 1: Trees and rivers everything represents the interdependence of humans upon nature. It represents the importance given by the indigenous people to the nature through their culture.
- Respondent 2: The story represents nature-culture through the motif of baskets. But it also conveys it through the interconnectedness of the society and how it derives strength and prosperity from the benevolence of the nature around it. Tree symbolizes nature.
- Respondent 3: Seasons symbolize her change of mental state. Canoes, fishing trip, and firewood gathering are the signs of nature-culture. The basket gives her hope to live which also symbolizes nature-culture.
- Respondent 4: The birch basket represents nature-culture as it is a sign of the widow's will to live while her husband's belongings represent the loss of the loved one and the burden of being a single parent.
- Respondent 5: The art of weaving birch tree baskets that the tree had taught the woman went on to become an important symbol of the culture of the people and is passed on until this day.
- Respondent 6: Tribal ethnic communities have always lived in close union through nature. The same nature that took away the woman's husband is also seen as a source of knowledge in the later part of the society.
- Respondent 7: The birch basket represents nature-culture as it is a sign of the widow's will to live. It talks about interconnectedness of the society.
- Respondent 8: The birch baskets represented a new means of living for the single mother in the society who is otherwise stuck in sorrow because of her dead husband. It represents the widow's will to live by her husband's belongings to the loss of loved one and the burden of being a single parent.

- Respondent 9: The birch basket represents nature-culture as it is a sign of the widow's will to live while her husband's belongings represent the loss of the loved one and the burden of being a single parent.
- Respondent 10: The birch baskets represented a new means of living for the single mother in the society who is otherwise stuck in sorrow because of her dead husband.

X Some of the titles suggested by the participants for the Anishinaabe folktale were:

- Respondent 1:   Tree the Savior
- Respondent 2:   The Basket of Life
- Respondent 3:   Into the Nature
- Respondent 4:   Grandmother Birch
- Respondent 5:   Mother Nature: The Life Giver
- Respondent 6:   Boats to Baskets
- Respondent 7:   The Cauldron of Life
- Respondent 8:   The Gift of Nature
- Respondent 9:   Under the Birch Tree
- Respondent 10:   Bound by Birch

The first three dimensions of the ecofemiotic framework namely spatio-temporal relativity, nature-cultural density, and spirituo-physical gravity contribute to Socio-Economic Parity characterized by wellbeing and balance at different levels of our cosmos. "The process by which individuals learn the culture of their society is known as socialization" (Haralambos and Holborn 6). In the past, folktales were used as cultural tools in the process of socialization. In the history of the planet the human beings came much late, yet they act as masters of the universe.

Socio-Economic Parity

Akam as a Zen-Deep Ecology interface suggests what Thich Nhat Hanh would state, "without minerals, plants and animals, how can there be human beings? If you remove or return all these elements, a human being cannot exist anymore. And yet we seek to protect and defend ourselves by destroying our non-us elements, including other species" (Thich Nhat Hanh 23). Hence it is important to evolve a socio-economic model that is rooted in love, compassion, and care.

The Earth Charter advocates the following principles: respect and care for the community of life; ecological integrity; social and economic justice; democracy, nonviolence, and peace. The identification of folktales as Gaia Care Narratives using the proposed theory promises "democratic societies that are just, participatory, sustainable, and peaceful" and ways to "secure Earth's bounty and beauty for present and future generations" (Web). According to the Earth Charter one of the ways of establishing ecological integrity is to "recognize and preserve the traditional knowledge and spiritual wisdom in all cultures that contribute to environmental protection and human wellbeing" (Web). Gaia Care Narratives challenge socio-economic inequality and create avenues toward equality, visualize a world of equity by providing narratives as custom tools that identify and address inequality, and offer systemic solutions to the systemic problems in order to bring about parity and justice.

Socio-Economic Parity can be reinstated by the integration of Gaia Care Narratives with the earth-centered socio-economic theories such as Gift Economy and Doughnut Economy. The recognition of the contribution of women and men who are involved in their household work reflects Genevieve Vaughan's concept of Gift Economy in this study. In an interview by Prof Rajani Kanth (January 2018) Genevieve Vaughan explains that "A Gift Economy is the material interaction of a community based on the direct provisioning of needs without the mediation of exchange" (Web). In the proposed framework, the nature-centered socio-economic theories, in other words the nature, are problematized and examined through the ecofemiotic framework in the Anishinaabe folktale.

According to Kate Raworth the twentieth-century economy relies on the wellbeing of the planet. In her article, "Kate Raworth-Doughnut Economics: Seven Ways to Think Like a 21st Century Economist", Florian Ross discusses the sustainable model of Doughnut economy and identifies seven ways of sustainable development and wellbeing. They are: (1) Change the goal to take care of "our planet's needs and to live in balance with our environment" (83); (2) see the big picture, "it is time to draw the economy in a new way, where it is embedded in larger systems like the society, the earth or the solar system with the goal to put it in service to life" (83); (3) nurture human nature to create "safe and just space" (83); (4) get savvy with systems where, "21st century economists do not see themselves as engineers who control the economy, but as gardeners who take care and shape it" (84); (5) design to distribute in order to "decrease economic inequalities" (84) and add "more equality when distributing their created values" (84); (6) create to regenerate, "the environmental damage is a result of a degenerative orientation of the industry and that we need a new economical thinking in the next century, which has a regenerative orientation and a more circular approach" (84); (7) be agnostic with growth where "the traditional economists regard constant economic growth as essential, but in nature nothing grows infinitely". We have to realize that the economic growth must eventually reach a limit. Kate Raworth suggests that the traditional exponential growth curve has to be replaced by the *s* curve, focusing on a level where we can cover both, our as well as our planet's needs to live in harmony with our environment. The proposed framework invokes identification of different types of motifs in the Anishinaabe folktale which includes time, seasons, space, elements, directions, land, water, flora, fauna, totem, lifeworld, divinity, love, motherhood, sisterhood, kinship, and sharing.

During the pre-industrial times people in a society believed in kinship and community living.

Classes did not exist since all members of society shared the same relationship to the forces of production. Every member was both producer and owner, all provided labor power and shared the products of their labor. Hunting and gathering is a subsistence economy which means that production only meets basic survival needs. Classes emerge when the productive capacity of society expands beyond the level required for subsistence. This occurs when agriculture becomes the dominant mode of production.

(Haralambos and Holborn 47)

Women and children suffer the most in the patriarchal consumerist mechanistic society. Vandana Shiva in her book *Ecofeminism* refers to Ruth Sidel's book *Women and Children Last* which gives an account of the unsinkable Titanic. Vandana Shiva explains:

The state of the global economy is in many ways comparable to the Titanic glittering and affluent and considered unsinkable. But as Ruth Sidel observed, despite our side-walk cafes, our saunas, our luxury boutiques, we, too, lack lifeboats for everyone where disaster strikes. Like the Titanic, the global economy has too many locked gates, segregated decks and policies ensuring that women and children will be first-not to be saved, but to fall into the abyss of poverty.

(Mies and Shiva 70)

Though economy and ecology emerged from the Greek word "Oikos" meaning "home" or "household" humans have severed the connection long ago. In order to re-establish the intricate connection between ecology and economy it is important to revisit the systems rooted in reductionism and mechanistic outlook, systems that hinder holistic growth, and systems that oppress the poor, the marginalized, and the other in a society. One way of doing it is to reweave the environmental imagination with the spirit of interconnectedness, interdependence, and intrinsic value of life.

As Gaia Care Narratives, folktales help us to reform social structures based on gift economy and philanthropic outlook. Gift economy is built upon goodwill and the ecological value of care and compassion. This helps the human race to restore earth's balance by countering the anthropocentric, androcentric perspectives dominant in our society and culture. This consciousness-raising process contributes to emergence. As Stephan Harding put it,

when we focus on relationships between the parts rather than on the parts in isolation, we very quickly encounter the principle of emergence, in which surprising properties appear at the level of the whole that cannot be understood through focusing on the parts alone.

(32)

By creating avenues toward socio-economic emergence, it is also possible to tackle ecological emergency. Through such eco-sophical journeys of storytelling it is possible to renew Gaia's future through reflective thoughts and responsible action.

The eco-storytelling session promoted multiple viewpoints and a pluralistic outlook. The storytelling process inspired "Care for the person" which indicated respect for the individual viewpoints; "Care for the persons around" which included teamwork and collaborative learning; "Care for others" which reflected the holistic development of the students and their role as future leaders for the wellbeing of the marginalized and the oppressed in the society and fourthly, "care for the environment" or wellbeing of the planet. Paulo Freire's idea of "dialogics" is identified as a major guiding principle in this study. In Paulo Freire's problem-posing education, "through dialogue, the teacher-of-the-students and the students-of-the-teacher cease to exist and a new term emerges; teacher-student with student-teachers" (Freire 80). In the eco-storytelling sessions "no one teaches another, nor is anyone self-taught. People teach each other, mediated by the world by the cognizable objects which in banking education are 'owned' by the leader" (Freire 80). They consider "dialogue" as a central element of cognition and skill development.

Eco-storytelling as a dialogic pedagogy provides a conducive platform where "subjectivity and objectivity are in constant dialectical relationship" (Freire 50). The young participants of the eco-storytelling process are conscious of the needs of the future generation. They believe in sustainable development which is "development which meets the needs of the present generation, without compromising the ability of future generations to meet their own needs" (Giddens and Sutton 188). The stories are potent tools nurtured by both the subjectivity and the objectivity of the conscious participants. As Freire explains,

> To deny the importance of subjectivity in the process of transforming the world and history is naïve and simplistic. It is to admit the impossible: a world without people. This objectivistic position is as ingenuous as that of subjectivism, which postulates people without a world. World and human beings do not exist apart from each other, they exist in constant interaction.
>
> (50)

The eco-storytelling sessions: help the students to become sensitive and conscious to the needs of the environment and the people around them; the system endorses co-intentional education-the "tutor-learner" and the "learner-tutor" as subjects; the process "humanizes" the tutor-learner and learner-tutor; it promotes dialogue and recognizes multiple perspectives; it helps the participants to identify problem-solving strategies through listening and telling tales; it encourages an on-going process of cognition for the participants; it motivates the participants to offer a "critical intervention" of reality; it facilitates care for the individual needs and respect for unique circumstances and concerns; the process promotes blending of theory and practice (praxis). Four Arrows provides a worldview chart that acts as a continuum in understanding the common dominant worldview manifestations and common indigenous worldview manifestations. Through eco-storytelling the two types of worldviews are integrated by the educator's worldview and the educated's worldview through the eco-pedagogical process. According to the theory of ecological modernization, five social and institutional structures need to be ecologically transformed: science and technology with sustainable technologies, markets and economic agents with environmental outcomes, nation-states to shape market conditions, social movements to guide humans in an ecological direction, ecological ideologies to persuade humans to get involved in the ecological modernization of a society (Giddens 191–92). The eco-storytelling process considers these five dimensions as sociological signposts in examining the scope of folktales as Gaia Care Narratives.

As a result, *Akaram* as a tool for socio-cultural-geographic-economic-linguistic understanding explicates: that human beings are endowed with special blessings to understand and revere the sacredness/intrinsic value of life on this planet and the larger universe; human action has an impact on the environment; there is a direct connection among the heart (*Akam*), the home (*Akam*), and the planet (*Akam*) which networks with *Puram* through the process of *Akaram*; when nature is embedded in culture, the culture is marked by interconnectedness and interdependence of life forms. As *Akam* fortifies the dynamics of *Puram*, *Akaram* forms a holistic way of understanding the larger universe. *Akaram* differs from an education that "is suffering from narration sickness" of the teacher where his/her task was "to fill the students with the contents of his narration-contents which are detached from reality, disconnected from the totality that engendered them and could give them significance" (Freire 71). The learners are no longer "containers" (Freire 72) or "receptacles" (Freire 72) to be "filled by the teacher" (Freire 72). In the proposed problem-posing method of eco-pedagogy the educator attempts to "re-form his/her reflections in the reflection of the students. The students are no longer docile listeners-are now critical co-investigators in dialogue with the teacher" (Freire 81).

As Paulo Freire explains in a dialogic pedagogy,

> the teacher presents the material to the students for their consideration, and re-considers her earlier. The role of the problem-posing educator is to

create; together with the students, the conditions under which knowledge at the level of the *doxa* is superseded by true knowledge, at the level of the *logos*.

(81)

The study confirms that the storytelling sessions as a form of eco-pedagogy that promote care for the viewpoints and opinion of people around them and as a result, they contribute toward a holistic development of the individuals that in turn would define their conscientious role and responsibility in their society and the environment at large. The storytelling sessions acquired a greater significance when the people came up with their interpretations and viewpoints that were nature-centric and upheld the different themes of abundance, benevolence, interconnectedness, interdependence, intrinsic value, and emergence.

The study throws light upon the systemic problems that exist in our society and our environment. By identifying folktales as Gaia Care Narratives, it is possible to reverse the systemic problems and offer systemic solutions for sustainable living: the systemic problems such as global warming, climate change, toxic wastes, loss of land, species and wilderness, disturbance to indigenous people, malnutrition, scarcity, sanitation, poverty, exploitation, maldevelopment, and genetic engineering. They happen because of reductionism, fragmentation, consumerism, commodification, insensitivity, selfishness, and greed.

Socio-economic parity manifests into eco-emergence in the folktales as Gaia Care Narratives with the following principles: Folktales reinforce the simplicity as a way of life to challenge the consumerist outlook. They revitalize abundance as a way of countering the worldview of scarcity and greed. They help us remodel alternative worldviews to suit the needs of the needy. By restructuring deep networks that promote circular sustainable economy folktales pave alternative path toward socio-economic balance. The folktales accentuate the process of reclaiming intrinsic creativity of humans to find systemic solutions. Differing from the mainstream worldviews, the earth-centered folktales help us to rethink collective identity and cooperation to face the socio-economic crisis. It provides us an opportunity to reform social structures based on gift economy and humanitarian outlook. It quintessentially tries to restore earth's balance by countering the anthropocentric, androcentric outlook among the humans. By re-visioning emergence of networks to tackle ecological emergency, the folktales help us to renew Gaia's future through reflective thoughts and responsible action.

The next chapter includes the summing up, findings of the study, scope and recommendations for future study, and conclusion.

Conclusion
Multiverse in a Grain

These opening four lines from the poem "Auguries of Innocence" by William Blake sum up the concept of *Tinai* in Tamil *Cankam* literature. A mother sees a universe in a grain. She nourishes and cares for the little seed which turns out to be a large Banyan tree or a fine human being. Most of the socio-economic-political-environmental-cultural problems of today are caused by one crucial man-made blunder in the human history, the silencing of women and other marginalized groups. In a world that is suffering because of the arrogance of human race and their thirst to conquer the planet, this study aims to explore nature-centered *Akam* signs of humility and humanity in Gaia Care Narratives that promote sustainable living and peaceful coexistence.

The book provides an integrated eco-pedagogical framework called ecofemiotics to understand and examine the earth-centered patterns in folktales as Gaia Care Narratives. It draws inspiration from the classical Tamil concept of *Akam* that is characterized by the different aspects of space-time, nature-culture, and spirit-matter. This contributes to an understanding of an alternative socio-economic order.

The proposed ecofemiotic model is characterized by three significant dimensions namely spatio-temporal relativity, nature-cultural density, and spirituo-physical gravity. These three dimensions are identified in the earth-centered folktales to form Gaia Care Narratives.

Space and time act as inseparable entities in the natural world. It connects the past, present, and the future. It draws the connection between events and the continuum. The recognition of flora, fauna, and the lifeworld contributes to the interdependence of nature-culture. The respect for the intrinsic value of life contributes to the understanding of spirit-matter connection. And together these three dimensions contribute to social, economic, and environmental justice.

The organic connection between space and time is understood in terms of interconnectedness and cyclical pattern of life. The folktales represent a microcosm and uphold the interconnections and the idea of "interbeing" as *Akam* or "heart, hearth and the Earth". The symbiotic connection between nature and culture is studied in relation to interdependence. The close proximity among the flora, fauna, and the lifeworld is visualized as "the embryo in

DOI: 10.4324/9781003406686-6

the womb" that offers hope to the future generations. The inherent connection between spirit and matter helps us to map the mindscape with the storyscape and the larger earthscape.

In conclusion, *Akam* as an eco-theory helps us to revisit the folktales using the green lens. *Akaram* as an eco-space provides us an opportunity to return to the roots and revive life-affirming motifs and patterns in earth-centered folktales. It emphasizes recoding of Gaia Motifs and Patterns with mindful mapping and storytelling. Recreating Gaia Care Narratives as consciousness-raising environmental discourse is the need of the hour. It is made possible by reengineering the Anthropocene with the time-tested toolkit of the indigenous people who lived close to nature. Reacclimatizing to the needs of the planet and the life forms in distress is a predominant concern of the environmental thinkers in the era of insensitivity and indifference. It is possible to realign with the space-time of Gaia or Mother Earth through indigenous belief systems and practices.

Folktales as Gaia Care Narratives help us to reconnect nature and culture as the fundamental principle of life's existence. By revisualizing space-time as an organic entity humans can connect with the environment in different ways. The ecofemiotic study attempts to reweave spirit and matter as the way out of the ecological chaos that exists in our society and culture. It helps us humans to rebuild our society and economy for a balanced planet. By doing this it is possible to reverse systemic problems through a systemic approach to mindful thinking and action. Folktales as Gaia Care Narratives help us to redial circular patterns as a way of overcoming the domination, destruction, and disintegration. The ecofemiotic study throws light upon the characteristics of systems thinking such as interconnections in a circular pattern, mapping and synthesis instead of analysis and fragmentation, emergence in contrast to silos, and studying causality in an interconnected system. Through storytelling it is possible to reconstruct earth designs based on nature-centered motifs and patterns. This is done by rewiring the dots, reviewing the storyscape, reinventing the mindscape, reshaping eco-cognition, and reviving the earthscape.

By redeeming nature's patterns through ecofemiotics and eco-pedagogy, it is possible to reaffirm the proximity of nature-culture. Stories as Gaia Care Narratives motivate us to revisit culture of nature and redefine nature of culture. Understanding nature-culture in folktales helps us to resist materialism and domination. By reassessing nature-centrism folktales provide avenues to regenerate an earth-centric lifeworld. By regulating the use of resources, it is possible to recover our planet. People who live close to nature lead a simple life and their stories help us to return to the Basics. Through ecofemiotics, folktales as Gaia Care Narratives help us to reinvent and re-join the sacredness of life. The act of storytelling helps us to revalue intrinsic worth, reawaken eco-consciousness, and renew our earth family. Stories initiate the process of revisualizing and remodeling alternative worldviews into the mainstream. Folktales help us to unravel and restructure deep networks.

By reconciling with earth spirituality, the storyteller and the told, the teacher and the student learn to respect our Mother Earth. Through the process of storytelling as dialogic pedagogy and through the identification of the eight types of *akam* namely: celebrative *akam*, divisive *akam*, passive *akam*, oppressive *akam*, interactive *akam*, collaborative *akam*, transformative *akam*, and regenerative *akam*, discordant notes are retuned into ecological harmony. For children who are nurtured by bedtime and mealtime, stories can boost their self-esteem, cultivate creativity and imagination, and instill faith in autonomy and collective strength. Folktales reinforce simplicity, revitalize abundance, and reimagine benevolence. The green folktales reverberate with motifs and patterns that build up intrinsic creativity in individuals as well as a group. This motivates us to rethink collective identity, reform social structures, and restore earth's balance; Gaia Care Narratives are a way of reexamining sustenance. Folktales that resonate earth's philosophy help us to reassure interconnectedness, reconsider interdependence, revision ecological and social emergence through abundance, and renew Gaia's Future.

The findings of the study are summed up by the systemic Gaia Care Principles that can be used as tools of consciousness-raising in creating awareness in the areas of society, culture, environment, and education. In her book *Nature, Culture and Gender: Re-reading the Folktale* published by Routledge in 2016, the author has identified the concept of *Terra Mater Lexis* "as the use of vocabulary that motivates care for Mother Earth and realization of interdependence of life" (52). Words with the prefix "Re-" as in Gloria Feman Orenstein's "Reweaving the World" and Cassandra Kircher's "rethinking dichotomies" (Gaard 159) are categorized as Terra Mater Lexis. Drawing a leaf out of this concept, Gaia Care Principles begin with the life-affirming action words with the prefix "Re-" to bring about environmental and social change.

Gaia Care Principles

I Spatio-Temporal Relativity promotes Interconnectedness

- Principle 1 – Revisualizing nature-centered space-time over human view of space and time
- Principle 2 – Revisiting nature's patterns to identify and integrate synchronous networks
- Principle 3 – Relinking the dots that work toward the wellbeing of all life forms on earth
- Principle 4 – Reconciling with our planet as integrated and significant parts of the whole
- Principle 5 – Reviewing the storyscape as a way of understanding indigenous wisdom
- Principle 6 – Reviving the earthscape through storytelling as environmental discourse

- Principle 7 – Redialing circular principles by interrogating binaries and linear patterns
- Principle 8 – Reversing systemic problems that oppress environment and the marginalized
- Principle 9 – Reassuring interconnectedness by challenging fragmentation and reductionism
- Principle 10 – Reconstructing earth designs that work in favor of sustainability and balance

II   Naturo-Cultural Density upholds Interdependence

- Principle 11 – Redeeming nature's motifs in life-affirming cultural narratives
- Principle 12 – Reaffirming nature-culture by examining mutuality among life forms
- Principle 13 – Re-reading inherent culture among the nonhuman beings in nature
- Principle 14 – Redefining the nature of a new regenerative earth-centric culture
- Principle 15 – Regulating the use of resources by understanding the needs of the environment
- Principle 16 – Regenerating earth-centric lifeworld by understanding interrelationships
- Principle 17 – Reimagining benevolence as a way out of ecological chaos and misery
- Principle 18 – Reexamining sustenance from the point of view of the marginalized
- Principle 19 – Reconsidering interdependence as a path toward sustainable living
- Principle 20 – Resonating earth's philosophy in different aspects of human culture

III   Spirituo-Physical Gravity emphasizes Intrinsic Value

- Principle 21 – Reinventing the mindscape to explore eco-sensitivity and eco-spirituality
- Principle 22 – Re-shaping eco-cognition to challenge and counter materialistic outlook
- Principle 23 – Resisting dominant systems that treat earth and the marginalized as matter
- Principle 24 – Re-joining sacredness as a way out of the global challenges that oppress life
- Principle 25 – Retuning discordant notes into harmonious tunes in accord with nature
- Principle 26 – Reconciling with earth spirituality to recreate a culture of love and care

- Principle 27 – Returning to the basics and rebuilding elements of sacredness in everyday life
- Principle 28 – Reawakening eco-consciousness among children and youth for a better future
- Principle 29 – Revaluing intrinsic worth of nonhuman living beings and the environment
- Principle 30 – Renewing the earth family with respect, compassion, and stewardship

IV Socio-Economic Parity contributes to Eco-Emergence

- Principle 31 – Reinforcing simplicity as a way of life to challenge the consumerist outlook
- Principle 32 – Revitalizing abundance to counter the worldview of scarcity and greed
- Principle 33 – Remodeling alternative worldviews to suit the needs of the needy
- Principle 34 – Restructuring deep networks that promote circular sustainable economy
- Principle 35 – Reclaiming intrinsic creativity of humans to find systemic solutions
- Principle 36 – Rethinking collective identity and cooperation to face the socio-economic crisis
- Principle 37 – Reforming social structures based on gift economy and humanitarian outlook
- Principle 38 – Restoring earth's balance by countering the anthropocentric, androcentric outlook
- Principle 39 – Revisioning emergence of networks to tackle ecological emergency
- Principle 40 – Renewing Gaia's future through reflective thoughts and responsible action

The research raises a number of pertinent questions, suggestions, and recommendations which can be considered for future study. To list a few:

- How do we counter resource depletion by reading a fable on contentment?
- How do we lessen the harmful effects of global warming through parables of simplicity and sensitivity?
- How do we understand "nature" as living forces rather than inert matter through legends?
- How do we learn the harmful effects of industrialization and pollution through consciousness-raising anecdotes?
- How do we examine the dynamics of earthquakes and tsunamis through ancient myths?

- How do we challenge deforestation and promote afforestation using tree stories?
- How do we explore water scarcity through river lore and ocean narratives?
- How do we study food security by telling tales of fasting, feasting, and sharing?
- How do we discourage throw-away societies by tales of inherent worth and intrinsic value?
- How do we counter consumerism through tales of eco-spirituality?
- How do we lessen the anthropogenic climate change through tales of deep ecological reflection and affirmative action?

Gaia Care Principles can be used as consciousness-raising tools in environmental activism through inter-semiotic translation. As a cyclical method the Gaia Care Principles can be used in the eco-pedagogy encouraging the learners to narrate tales of their own based on environmental imagination and reality. Similarly, the eight types of *akam* namely celebrative *akam*, divisive *akam*, passive *akam*, oppressive *akam*, interactive *akam*, collaborative *akam*, transformative *akam*, and regenerative *akam* in a folktale or a literary text can be explored through the presences and absences of Gaia Care Principles.

Each Gaia Care Principle can be taken in isolation and studied in relation to alternative worldviews across cultures, societies, and economies. Alternatively, Gaia Care Principles can be used as signposts in fieldwork where case studies and surveys are done on society and environment. Gaia Care Principles can be used as a foundation to bring about green agricultural, technological reforms such as organic and sustainable farming; tapping clean, efficient, abundant, and renewable energy resources; promoting rotation of crops, agroecology/agroforestry, diversification of farming systems, sustainable agriculture; inventing eco-designs using bio-mimicry; aiming at zero waste/zero emissions; creating eco-Villages/eco-Cities; building green architecture; and promoting solar energy conservation and permaculture.

Primarily, the use of folklore as Gaia Care Narrative is envisioned as a form of Eco literacy in the classrooms as *Akaram*, a conscientious space of consciousness-raising. By revisiting the indigenous knowledge systems, the eco-storyteller creates avenues toward alternative worldviews that interrogate the systemic problems that occur in our contemporary society and the world at large. Folktales as Gaia Care Narratives not only offer consolation in times of strife, but they also inspire creativity and imagination in the minds of humans to identify ways to solve ecological and economic problems. Creative works of art, photography, and films can be inspired by folktales as Gaia Care Narratives.

Likewise, films can be read as Gaia Care Narratives through the ecofemiotic framework. Painting, photography, and other forms of visual art can be mapped using the proposed framework to study the spatio-temporal relativity, nature-cultural density, spirituo-physical gravity, and socio-economic parity to form Gaia Care Narratives. The study conforms to the mapping of folktales as educational tools in eco-pedagogy. Folk songs, proverbs, and riddles can also be mapped using the framework. Earth-centered poetry, short stories, novels, and drama can provide ample scope for the recognition of the spatio-temporal relativity, nature-cultural density, spirituo-physical gravity, and socio-economic parity to form Gaia Care Narratives. Gaia Care Narratives can also be generated through fieldwork and case studies. From a socioeconomic perspective the different aspects of space-time, nature-culture, and spirit-matter contribute to socio-economic parity.

To conclude, Gaia Care Narratives in eco-pedagogy promote deep understanding and awareness of the environment around us. It believes in deep questioning and interrogation of the systemic problems that happen around us. It also believes in deep commitment toward the wellbeing of the Earth Mother or Gaia through the act of cognition, perception, consciousness-raising, networking, and emergence. This is facilitated by the process of reweaving Gaia Care Narratives. They emerge as counter-narratives to the descent narratives of global warming, climate change, pollution, and deforestation. Human beings must let go of their avarice and greed they wish to take by contributing to the disintegration of the planet and adopt simplicity and contentment as a way to promote regeneration of life on Earth. Humans carry authentic words in their *Akam* that can quintessentially germinate into conscientious action. They form seeds of creation where the storyteller and the told form parts of the whole in radically reshaping the *Akam* of humans for the wellbeing of the planet.

References

Works Cited

Balakrishnan, Jayanthashri, editor. 2013. *Kuruntokai*. Central Institute of Classical Tamil.

Brown, J. Stephen. 1965. *The World of Imagery: Metaphor and Kindred Imagery*. Haskell House.

Buell, Lawrence. 1995. *The Environmental Imagination: Thoreau, Nature Writing and the Foundation of American Culture*. Harvard UP.

Capra, Fritjof. 1997. *The Web of Life*. Anchor.

———. 2007. *The Tao of Physics*. HarperCollins.

Capra, Fritjof, and Pier Luigi Luisi. 2014. *The Systems View of Life – A Unifying Vision*. Cambridge UP.

Carson, Rachel. 2000. *Silent Spring*. Penguin books ltd.

Clark, Timothy. 2011. *The Cambridge Introduction to Literature and the Environment*. Cambridge UP.

Devy, G.N., editor. 2002. *Painted Words: An Anthology of Tribal Literature*. Penguin Books Ltd.

Diamond, Irene, and Gloria Feman Orenstein, editor. 1990. *Reweaving the World: The Emergence of Ecofeminism*. Sierra Club Books.

Doerfler, Jill et al., editors. 2013. *Centering Anishinaabeg Studies: Understanding the World Through Stories*. Michigan State UP, East Lansing and U of Manitoba P.

Freire, Paulo. 2018. *Pedagogy of the Oppressed*. 50th Anniversary edition. Bloomsburry Academic.

Gaard, Greta, editor. 1993. *Ecofeminism: Women, Animals, Nature*. Temple UP.

Gaard, Greta, and Patrick D. Murphy, editors. 1998. *Ecofeminist Literary Criticism: Theory, Interpretation, Pedagogy*. U of Illinois P.

Giddens, Anthony, and Philips W. Sutton. 2017. *Sociology*. 8th edition. Polity.

Glotfelty, Cheryll, editor. 1996. *The Ecocriticism Reader*. Georgia UP.

Gottlieb, S. Roger. 2004. *This Sacred Earth: Religion, Nature, Environment*. Routledge.

Haralambos, M., and R.M. Holborn. 2018. *Sociology: Themes and Perspectives*. Oxford UP.

Harding, Stephan. 2006. *Animate Earth – Science, Intuition and Gaia*. Chelsea Green Publishing Company.

Ingram, Annie Merill et al., editors. 2007. *Coming into Contact: Explorations in Ecocritical Theory and Practice*. Georgia UP.

Lovelock, James. 2016. *Gaia: A New Look at Life on Earth*. Oxford UP.

Macdonald, Margaret Read. 2005. *Earth Care: World Folktales to Talk About*. August House Inc.

Maran, Timo, and Kalevi Kull. 2014. "Ecosemiotics: Main Principles and Current Developments." *Geografiska Annaler: Series B, Human Geography*, vol. 96.

McAfee, Noelle. 2004. *Julia Kristeva*. Routledge.

McKay, F. Helen. 2001. *Gadi Mirrabooka: Australian Aboriginal Tales from the Dreaming*. Greenwood Publishing Group, Inc.

Mies, Maria, and Vandana Shiva. 2010. *Ecofeminism*. Rawat Publications.

Murugan, V., translator. 2000. *Tolkāppiyam in English: Translation, with the Tamil Text, Transliteration in the Roman Script, Introduction, Glossary, and Illustrations*. Institute of Asian Studies.

Naess, Arne. 1990. *Ecology, Community and Lifestyle: Outline of an Ecosophy*. Cambridge UP.

Nhat Hanh, Thich. 2021. *Zen and the Art of Saving the Planet*. Penguin Random House.

Orenstein, Gloria Feman, editor. 1990. *Reweaving the World: The Emergence of Ecofeminism*. Sierra Club Books.

Ortner, Sherry B. 1974. "Is Female to Male as Nature Is to Culture?" *Woman, Culture, and Society*, edited by M.Z. Rosaldo and L. Lamphere. Stanford UP.

Porselvi, Mary Vidya. 2016. *Nature, Culture and Gender: Rereading the Folktale*. Routledge.

———. 2017. *Sylvan Tones: English Through Folklore*. Macmillan.

Ramanujan, A.K., translator. 2006. *Poems of Love and War*. Oxford UP.

Sebeok, Thomas A. 2001. *Signs: An Introduction to Semiotics*. U of Toronto P.

Siewers, Alfred Kentigern, editor. 2014. *Re-Imagining Nature: Environmental Humanities and Ecosemiotics*. Bucknell UP.

Slovic, Scott. 1992. *Seeking Awareness in American Nature Writing*. U of Utah P.

Steiner, Frederick. 2016. *Human Ecology – How Nature and Culture Shape Our World*. Island Press.

Tuan, Yi-Fu. 1974. *Topophilia: A Study of Environmental Perception, Attitudes and Values*. Prentice-Hall.

Wilson, O. Edward. 2016. *Half-Earth: Our Planet's Fight for Life*. Liveright Publishing Corporation.

Zimmerman, J. Larry. 2011. *The Sacred Wisdom of the Native Americans*. Chartwell Books.

Zvelebil, Kamil. 1986. *Literary Conventions in Akam Poetry*. Institute of Asian Studies.

Web Resources

Blake, William. "Auguries of Innocence." Web. 16 Apr. 2021. https://www.poetryloverspage.com/poets/blake/to_see_world.html.

Cherokee Tale. "The Tale of Two Wolves." Web. 14 Apr. 2020. https://www.nanticokeindians.org/page/tale-of-two-wolves.

The Earth Charter. Web. 18 Apr. 2022. https://earthcharter.org/read-the-earth-charter/.

Four Arrows. "Indigenous Worldview." Web. 20 Feb. 2022. https://www.kindredmedia.org/glossary/indigenous-worldview/.

Giono, Jean. "The Man Who Planted Trees." Web. 30 Apr. 2022. https://www.arvindguptatoys.com/arvindgupta/plantedtrees.pdf.

Kanth, Rajani. "Ideas for Our Times: Interview-Genevieve Vaughan." Web. 20 July 2020. http://gift-economy.com/wordpress/wp-content/uploads/2018/02/IDEAS-FOR-OUR-TIMES-rev.pdf.

Quach, Phuong. "Coming Home." Web. 9 May 2022. https://www.resurgence.org/magazine/article5932-coming-home.html.

Raworth, Kate. "Doughnut Economics: Seven Ways to Think Like a 21st Century Economist." Web. 19 Mar. 2021. https://www.kateraworth.com/doughnut/.

Scharmer, Otto. "Vertical Literacy: Reimagining the 21st-Century University." Web. 17 Apr. 2022. https://medium.com/presencing-institute-blog/vertical-literacy-12-principles-for-reinventing-the-21st-century-university-39c2948192ee.

Selvamony, Nirmal. "Oikopoetics and Tamil Poetry." Web. 15 Sept. 2019. http://www.angelfire.com/nd/nirmaldasan/oikos.html.

Shiva, Vandana. "Forests and Freedom." 266, May–June 2011. Web. 19 Apr. 2022. http://www.resurgence.org/magazine/article3390.html.

Spanne, Autumn. 2021. "What Is Deep Ecology? Philosophy, Principles and Criticism. TreeHugger-Sustainability for All." Web. 14 Apr. 2022. https://www.treehugger.com/what-is-deep-ecology-philosophy-principles-and-criticism-5191550.

The Story of Ubuntu. Web. 14 Feb. 2020. https://synergyholistichealth.com/the-story-of-ubuntu/.

The Unicorn Song – Irish Folk Song. Web. 16 Mar. 2021. http://www.thebards.net/music/lyrics/The_Unicorn_Song.shtm.

Works Consulted

Adams, Carol, editor. 1993. *Ecofeminism and the Sacred*. The Continuum Publishing Company.

Altman, Irwin, and Martin M. Chemers. 1984. *Culture and Environment*. Cambridge UP.

Anand, Mulk Raj. 1974. *Folk Tales of Punjab*. Sterling Publishers.

Andrews, Jane. 2007. *The Stories Mother Nature Told Her Children*. Yesterday's Classics.

Bahadur, K.P. 1991. *Folk Tales of Uttar Pradesh*. Sterling Publishers.

Barry, Peter, and William Welstead. 2017. *Extending Ecocriticism: Crisis, Collaboration and Challenge in the Environmental Humanities*. Manchester UP.

Bates, Ulkii et al. 1995. *Women's Realities, Women's Choices*. Oxford UP.

Beauvoir, Simone De. 1988. *The Second Sex*. Trans. H. M. Prashley. Pan Books Ltd.

Bernstein, Basil. 1971. *Theoretical Studies Towards a Sociology of Language*. Routledge and Paul.

Bose, Tara. 1971. *Folk Tales of Gujarat*. Sterling Publishers.

Borgohein, B.K. 1974. *Folk Tales of Meghalaya and Arunachal Pradesh*. Sterling Publishers.

Borgohein, B.K., and Roy Chaudhury. 1975. *Folk Tales of Nagaland, Manipur, Tripura and Mizoram*. Sterling Publishers.

Braidotti, Rosi et al. 1994. *Women, the Environment and Sustainable Development: Towards a Theoretical Synthesis*. Zed Books.

Brown, Gillian, and George Yule. 2001. *Discourse Analysis*. Cambridge UP.

Buell, Lawrence. 2001. *Writing for an Endangered World*. The Belkaap of Harvard UP.

———. 2006. *The Future of Environmental Criticism – Environmental Crisis and Literary Imagination*. Blackwell Publishing Ltd.

Buzan, Tony, and Barry Buzan. 2010. *The Mind Map Book: Unlock Your Creativity, Boost Your Memory, Change Your Life*. Pearson Publishers.

Cameron, Deborah. 1993. *Feminism and Linguistic Theory*. Macmillan.

Chakravarti, Uma, and Preeti Gill, editors. 2001. *Shadow Lives: Writings on Widowhood*. Kali for Women.

Chandran, Satish. 1973. *Folk Tales of Karnataka*. Sterling Publishers.

Chaudhury, Bani Roy. 1969. *Folk Tales of Kashmir*. Sterling Publishers.

Chaudhury, Indhu Roy, and Veena Srivastava. 1991. *Folk Tales of Haryana*. Sterling Publishers.

Cheria, Anita et al. 2004. *A Human Rights Approach to Development: Resource Book*. Books for Change.

Corcoran, Peter Blaze, and James Wohlpart. 2008. *A Voice for Earth: American Writers Respond to the Earth Charter*. Georgia UP.

Coupe, Lawrence. 2000. *The Green Studies Reader: From Romanticism to Ecocriticism*. Routledge.

Detraz, Nicole. 2017. *Gender and the Environment*. Polity Press.

Dundes, Alan. 1990. *Essays in Folklore Theory and Method*. Cre-A.

———. 2005. *The Study of Folklore*. Prentice-Hall.

Fellows, Andrew. 2019. *Gaia, Psyche and Deep Ecology: Navigating Climate Change in the Anthropocene*. Routledge.

Fernando, Priyanthi, and Gina Porter, editors. 2002. *Balancing the Load: Women, Gender and Transport*. Zed Books.

Fontanille, Jacques. 2006. *The Semiotics of Discourse*. Peter Lang.

Franco, Fernando et al., editors. 2000. *The Silken Swing: The Cultural Universe of Dalit Women*. Stree.

Fuss, Diana. 1989. *Essentially Speaking: Feminism, Nature and Difference*. Routledge.

Garrard, Greg. 2004. *Ecocriticism*. Routledge.

———. editor. 2014. *The Oxford Handbook of Ecocriticism*. Oxford UP.

Haenn, Nora et al., editors. 2016. *The Environment in Anthropology – A Reader in Ecology, Culture and Sustainable Living*. New York UP.

Handoo, Jawaharlal, and Reimund Kvideland, editors. 1999. *Folklore in the Changing World*. Zooni Publications.

Hart, George. "On the Status of Tamil as a Classical Language." Web. 15 Apr. 2020. https://sangamtamilliterature.wordpress.com/dr-george-harts-letter-recommending-tamil-as-classical-language/.

Heise, Ursula K. 2006. *Greening English: Recent Introduction to Ecocriticism. Contemporary Literature*. U of Wisconsin P.

———. 2018. *Sense of Place and Sense of Planet: The Environmental Imagination of the Global*. Oxford UP.

Hiltner, Ken, editor. 2015. *Ecocriticism: The Essential Reader*. Routledge.

hooks, bell. 2000. *Feminist Theory: From Margin to Center*. Pluto Press.

Humphreys, Tony. 2002. *Self-Esteem: The Key to Your Child's Future*. Gill and Macmillan Ltd.

Jacob, K. 1972. *Folk Tales of Kerala*. Sterling Publishers.

Jeyaseelan, Thomas B. 2002. *Women Rights and Law*. Indian Social Institute.

Jha, Rajesh Kumar. 2010. *Women and Human Rights*. Mohit Books International.

Kamala, N., editor. 2009. *Translating Women: Indian Interventions*. Zubaan Books.

Karuppaian, V., and K. Parimurugan. 2001. *Tribal Ecology and Development*. Department of Anthropology, U of Madras.

Keller, Lynn. 2017. *Recomposing Ecopoetics: North American Poetry of the Self-Conscious Anthropocene*. Virginia UP.

Kothari, Rita. 2006. *Speech and Silence: Literary Journeys by Gujarati Women*. Zubaan Books.

Lee Mckay, Sandra, and Nancy H. Hornberger, ediors. 2006. *Sociolinguistics and Language Teaching*. Cambridge UP.

Lewis, John. 1984. *Anthropology Made Simple*. Heinemann.

Lovelock, James. 2006. *The Revenge of Gaia: Why the Earth Is Fighting Back – and How We Can Still Save Humanity*. Allen Lane.

———. 2009. *The Vanishing Face of Gaia: A Final Warning: Enjoy It While You Can*. Allen Lane.

Lourdu, T. 1997. *Nattar Valakkatriyal: Cila Atippataikal*. Folklore Resource and Research Centre.

Maathai, Wangari. 2006. *Unbowed: One Woman's Story*. William Heinemann.

Majumdar, Geeta. 1971. *Folk Tales of Bengal*. Sterling Publishers.

Maran, Timo. 2018. "Deep Ecosemiotics: Forest as a Semiotic Model." *RSSI*, vol. 38, no. 3; vol. 39, no. 1–2 (2019). Association canadienne de sémiotique/Canadian Semiotic Association.

McKibben, Bill, editor. 2008. *Environmental Writing Since Thoreau: American Earth*. The Library of America.

Merchant, Carolyn. 1981. *The Death of Nature: Women, Ecology and the Scientific Revolution*. Harper and Row.

Michael, E. Zimmerman et al., editors. 1993. *Environmental Philosophy: From Animal Rights to Radical Ecology*. Prentice-Hall.

Miri, Sujata. 2006. *Stories and Legends of the Liangmai Nagas*. National Book Trust.

Mitra, Debamitra, and Kasturi Basu, editors. 2009. *Ecofeminism: An Overview*. ICFAI UP.

Moe, M. Aaron. 2019. *Ecocriticism and the Poeisis of Form: Holding on to Proteus*. Routledge.

Mohanty, Chandra Talpade. 2003. *Feminism without Borders: Decolonizing Theory Practicing Solidarity*. Zubaan Books.

Monteith, Moira, editor. 1986. *Women's Writing: A Challenge to Theory*. The Harvester Press Ltd.

Mooney, Annabelle, and Betty Evans. 2007. *Globalization: The Key Concepts*. Routledge.

Naess, Arne. 1977. "Identification as a Source of Deep Ecological Attitudes." *Ethical Issues: Perspectives for Canadians*, edited by Eldon Soiffer. Okcir Press, pp. 83–93.

———. 1994. "Deep Ecology." *Key Concepts in Critical Theory: Ecology*, edited by Carolyn Merchant. Humanities Press, pp. 120–24.

———. 1996. "Living a Life That Reflects Evolutionary Insights." *Conservation Biology*, vol. 16, no. 6, pp. 1557–59.

Narasimhan, Sakuntala. 1999. *Empowering Women: An Alternative Strategy from Rural India*. Sage Publications.

Nhat Hanh, Thich. 1996. "This Sun My Heart." *Engaged Buddhist Reader: Ten Years of Engaged Buddhist Publishing*, edited by Arnold Kotler. Parallax Press, pp. 162–70.

Norris, Nanette, editor. 2013. *Words for a Small Planet: Ecocritical Views*. Lexington Books.

Pakrasi, Mira. 1969. *Folk Tales of Assam*. Sterling Publishers.

Parmar, S. 1973. *Folk Tales of Madhya Pradesh*. Sterling Publishers.

Philips, Dana. 1990. *The Truth of Ecology, Nature, Culture and Literature in America*. Oxford UP.

Pillai, Shanmugam. 2016. *Kuruntokai*. Maruthi Press.

Plant, Judith, ed. 1989. *Healing the Wounds: The Promise of Ecofeminism*. New Society.

Pretty, Jules. 2007. *The Earth Only Endures: On Reconnecting with Nature and our place in it*. London: Earthscan.

Raine, Anne. 2017. *"Ecocriticism and Modernism" the Oxford Handbook of Ecocriticism*. Edited by Greg Garrard. Oxford UP.

Rajanarayanan, Ki. 2009. *Where Are You Going You Monkeys? Folktales from Tamilnadu*. Blaft Publications.

Raju, B.R. 1974. *Folk Tales of Andhra Pradesh*. Sterling Publishers.

Rangarajan, Swarnalatha. 2018. *Ecocriticism: Big Ideas and Strategies*. Orient Blackswan.

Rosa Caldas-Coulthard, Carmen, and Malcolm Coulthard, editors. 1996. *Texts and Practices: Readings in Critical Discourse Analysis*. Routledge.

Sahi, Jyoti. 1994. *The Child and the Serpent: Reflections of Popular Indian Symbols*. Asian Trading Corporation.

Satterfield, Terry, and Scott Slovic. 2004. *What's Nature Worth? Narrative Expressions of Environmental Values*. U of Utah P.

Schliephake, Christopher. 2017. *Ecocriticism, Ecology and the Culture of Antiquity*. Lexington Books.

Seethalakshmi, K.A. 1969. *Folk Tales of Tamilnadu*. Sterling Publishers.

———. 1972. *Folk Tales of Himachal Pradesh*. Sterling Publishers.

Sheorey, I. 1973. *Folk Tales of Maharashtra*. Sterling Publishers.

Stein, Jane. 1997. *Empowerment and Women's Health: Theory, Methods and Practice*. Zed Books Ltd.

Stibbe, Arran, editor. 2009. *The Handbook of Sustainability Literacy: Skills for a Changing World*. Green Books Ltd.

Stubbs, M. 1983. *Discourse Analysis: The Sociolinguistic Analysis of Natural Language*. Basil Blackwell.

Sturgeon, Noel. 1997. *Ecofeminist Natures*. Routledge.

Takahashi, Takanobu. 1995. *Tamil Love Poetry and Poetics*. E.J. Brill.

Tamizh Annal. 1986. *Tolkappiyar's Poetics: Implied Meaning (Ullurai)*. Meenakshi Puthaka Nilayam.

Vakoch, A. Douglas, editor. 2012. *Feminist Ecocriticism: Environment, Women and Literature*. Lexington Books.

Vakoch, A. Douglas, and Sam Mickey, editors. 2018. *Literature and Ecofeminism – Intersectional and International Voices*. Routledge.

Wajnryb, Ruth. 2009. *Stories: Narrative Activities in the Language Classroom*. Cambridge UP.

Web Resources

Ashliman. "Androcles and the Lion – Aesop's Fable." Web. 17 Apr. 2022. http://www.pitt.edu/~dash/type0156.html#aesop1.

Chase, Christopher. "The Universe Is One Harmonious Whole." Web. 12 Aug. 2020. https://creativesystemsthinking.wordpress.com/2014/10/28/the-universe-is-one-harmonious-whole/.

Devi, Sarajubala, and Melissa Wallang. "Sustaining Cultural Values in Formal Education: Integration of Folktales in School Language Curriculum." *Language in India*, vol. 22, no. 3, Mar. 2022, pp. 110+. Gale Academic OneFile. Web. 1 May 2022. <www.link.gale.com/apps/doc/A700446363/AONE?u=ussd&sid=bookmark-AONE&xid=50a202a5>.

Diehm, Christian. "Arne Naess, Val Plumwood, and Deep Ecological Subjectivity: A Contribution to the 'Deep Ecology-Ecofeminism Debate'." *Ethics & the Environment*, vol. 7, no. 1, Jan. 2002, p. 24. Gale Academic OneFile. Web. 1 May 2022. <www.link.gale.com/apps/doc/A138483130/AONE?u=ussd&sid=bookmark-AONE&xid=6428c076>.

Donahue, Thomas J. "Anthropocentrism and the Argument from Gaia Theory." *Ethics & the Environment*, vol. 15, no. 2, Fall 2010, pp. 51+. Gale Academic OneFile. Web. 1 May 2022. <www.link.gale.com/apps/doc/A243714764/AONE?u=ussd&sid=bookmark-AONE&xid=3055da4b>.

Emerson, Ralph Waldo. "The Complete Works Vol X. Lectures and Biographical Sketches." Web. 28 Apr. 2022. https://www.bartleby.com/90/1005.html.

Forbes, Linda C., and Laura Sells. "Reorganizing the Woman/Nature Connection." *Organization & Environment*, vol. 10, no. 1, 1997, pp. 20–22. JSTOR. Web. 1 May 2022. <www.jstor.org/stable/26161651>.

Gifford, Terry. "Recent Critiques of Ecocriticism." *New Formations*, no. 64, Spring 2008, pp. 15+. Gale Academic OneFile. Web. 1 May 2022. <www.link.gale.com/apps/doc/A178452219/AONE?u=ussd&sid=bookmark-AONE&xid=25918423>.

Gregory, Julie, and Samah Sabra. "Engaged Buddhism and Deep Ecology: Beyond the Science/Religion Divide." *Human Architecture: Journal of the Sociology of Self-Knowledge*, vol. 6, no. 3, Summer 2008, pp. 51+. Gale Academic OneFile. Web. 2 May 2022. <www.link.gale.com/apps/doc/A227887835/AONE?u=ussd&sid=bookmark-AONE&xid=4fd72dde>.

Iskwew, Muskeke. "Grandmother's Creation Story – Cree Legend." Web. 16 Apr. 2018. http://www.indigenouspeople.net/whitwolf.htm.

Knyazeva, Helena. "Ecological Philosophy and Its Applications: Following Felix Guattari's Tradition." *Cosmos and History: The Journal of Natural and Social Philosophy*, vol. 17, no. 1, Jan. 2021, pp. 137+. Gale Academic OneFile. Web. 3 May 2022. <www.link.gale.com/apps/doc/A671307118/AONE?u=ussd&sid=bookmark-AONE&xid=9f6b55ca>.

Mckee, Andrew. "The Unicorn Song – Irish Folk Song." Web. 18 Nov. 2022. http://www.thebards.net/music/lyrics/The_Unicorn_Song.shtml.

Moolla, Zunaid. "Looking Ahead, and Aiming for a New Way of Life." *New Agenda: South African Journal of Social and Economic Policy*, no. 79, Mar. 2021, pp. 11+. Gale Academic OneFile. Web. 2 May 2022. <www.link.gale.com/apps/doc/A688765311/AONE?u=ussd&sid=bookmark-AONE&xid=2b6c7115>.

Rowe, J. Stan. "From Reductionism to Holism in Ecology and Deep Ecology." *The Ecologist*, vol. 27, no. 4, July–Aug. 1997, pp. 147+. Gale Academic OneFile. Web. 1 May 2022. <www.link.gale.com/apps/doc/A20191797/AONE?u=ussd&sid=book mark-AONE&xid=dcc45da6>.

Swanger, Joanna. "Women and the Gift Economy: A Radically Different World-view Is Possible." *Canadian Woman Studies*, vol. 26, no. 1, Winter–Spring 2007, pp. 106+. Gale Academic OneFile. Web. 2 May 2022. <www.link.gale.com/apps/ doc/A232179036/AONE?u=ussd&sid=bookmark-AONE&xid=cfc6c9bc>.

Zimmerman, Michael E. "Deep Ecology, Ecoactivism, and Human Evolution." *ReVision*, vol. 24, no. 4, Spring 2002, pp. 40+. Gale Academic OneFile. Web. 3 May 2022. <www.link.gale.com/apps/doc/A89380355/AONE?u=ussd&sid=bookmark-AONE& xid=8f2d36bd>.

Index

For Product Safety Concerns and Information please contact our EU
representative GPSR@taylorandfrancis.com
Taylor & Francis Verlag GmbH, Kaufingerstraße 24, 80331 München, Germany